My UFO.

by Philip Petersen

CHAPTER ONE

1. Foreword.

I am not a writer. There will be mistakes. I will repeat myself. I am trying to clear my conscience as I do not now want to leave this Earth having kept silent. At least putting this on paper I know that its out there so if no human bothers with it I can't be blamed. Things I learned on this particular day about fifteen years ago are now appearing! So maybe I was not hoaxed as the hoaxers could not have predicted what we have now and they certainly would not be employed as hoaxers and would be very rich indeed. Take the mobile phone. The one I had was big and only worked on the M1. The mobile devices

I saw beings carrying on the screen did everything just as tablet phones do today. I will tell you in these ramblings what I saw the mobile devices doing that we have not thought of yet. Transport. Nearly all other transport systems I saw were underground, small buggies running in air powered tubes, attaining insane speeds and transporting their owners to their destinations in minutes and the subject planet I was shown was a lot bigger than ours. I can explain how we have been visited thousands of times and why only very few people have been communicated to and not normally via a being, how people spotting UFOs have reported certain effects to which I now have plausible explanations. The device I was talking to only answered questions and did not ask me anything as it was really an elaborate version of the plaque on the side of the Voyager spacecraft that depicted humans and The Earth etc. This one opened the doors whilst it collected data in case an intelligent being happened across it. Unfortunately, in my case it didn't get anyone intelligent but only a being from this planet. I wasted lots of potential question time checking for anything that could show I was being hoaxed including shouting for Jeremy Beadle to show his face, trying to see if there were any wires leading away, looking for the Range Warden and carrying out my own experiments like pushing the whole craft about four inches and being shoved as if by an Elephant when it relocated. I learned how it collected data and distributed it, what it knew about this part of the universe, what had happened in other parts of the universe, what we should do to survive and like subjects. I asked lots of questions about Ancient Egypt and know what the Pyramids were really used for and why the Egyptian paintings / statues all have strange eyes.

So even if you are a UFO non-believer or still think the planet was created in seven days by your God, want to know what to do for your future, what is coming and how soon, how to build zero emission and zero carbon buildings, how to stop the banks and politicians ripping us off by eliminating them completely, the list is endless. Ah yes!   Where is the end of the universe ? Read on.

CHAPTER TWO

2. Run Up.

I was due to go to Edinburgh to pick up a directors car and drive it back to Milton Keynes and thought it would be a good idea to go to Otterburn Ranges to photograph the next lot of military vehicles that had been put on the ranges as targets. The car was to be sent for service at the company Jaguar dealer on the Monday so I had all weekend. Another chauffeur dropped me at Luton airport. All was uneventful and I found myself at the ranges just before Dark and I stopped in the entrance to the memorial where the Battle of Otterburn took place. The idea was to sleep in the car and see if there were any exercises going on that night and in which direction as another of my hobbies was to collect military odds for the Bletchley Park museum. I awoke in the morning and set off early. I went in the back way and not through the camp as I didn't have a permission letter from Col.Cross as I had done in the past. I did stick out like a sore thumb in a Jaguar but Otterburn is so big that you rarely meet anyone there anyway. I found the Ferret armoured cars I was looking for and ran into the Range Warden on his quad which is just what I didn't want to do. He knew me from previous visits and told me of a few more Ferrets which were rare Mk 5s with a flotation screen. I could not see them from where I parked the car so went to an old Centurion ARV and standing on top, could see three ferret turrets on top of a ridge. There was also something I thought at the time looked like a white metal corroded water tank. I had seen the dull silver unpainted hull of an experimental CVRT vehicle earlier in the day so seeing something dull grey among the green vehicles disarmed my surprise. I climbed to the ridge and as the warden had stated, there were the three Ferrets and a silver water tank. The tank was a lot bigger than I thought I had seen from the ARV and had a big square hole through the top half and no features whatsoever. Its finish was slightly rough and looked like aluminium that had been sprayed with a varnish which made it look darker. On closer inspection and after knocking on it to see if it were hollow, it felt thick like armour plate. It didn't give like aluminium so was thick. I was thinking what the material could be and lent on the edge with one elbow. I could feel a slight vibration. It was so slight that I put it down to wind vibrating the structure as it blew through the big square hole. The other thing bugging me was the fact that it had no legs. I had approached it thinking about the colour and material and subconsciously thought they were just rusty or painted black in the shadow of the tank. I went under and found no legs but assumed it was supported by something protruding from the bank as the far rim appeared to be resting on the bank behind. I went to have a look inside the square hole and could stand in this with about 40 cm to spare. There was a block on the floor up against the inner wall half way between both entrances and no other features. I was fast becoming sceptical about the water tank theory and sat on the block. The second I put my weight on the block the opposite wall came to life like a big TV screen but blank. About this time the biggest TV was about 26 inches so this was a shock and my theory fast turned to Army operations centre. There was nothing on the screen but if I made a noise a line appeared. I had got up a few times and inspected the wall which had gone off as I removed my weight from the block and it was the same material as the rest of the tank but noticeably smoother. The whole inside was of the same smoothness. The humming never ceased and to test my theory I rested my teeth on the rim like I used to do to see if something was still running. This confirmed something was on and I assumed it was a generator or something similar. Everything so far was possible on Earth so I had no reason to think space at this point. In fact, the whole session could have been thought up by pranksters and I was thinking if this were discarded military hardware, how good it would look at Bletchley Park on display as Col. Cross was known to donate rare items to museums if they wanted them. I don't like do disappoint but I saw no lights, no green men, no impossible aerobatics and actually never did. I'm thinking that after 15 odd years that if I write all this down a reader may make head or tail about what I learned that day. I most certainly do not want to die knowing that something in this book may be responsible for fast-forwarding the human race. Quite a few things I learned on that day have suddenly materialized which sealed the decision to put pen to paper.

I entered the top section again which was about 12-15 feet through the upper part of the tank and this you could walk right through and jump off the rim the other side. And sat on the block. The whole side wall came to life again and I talked. To cut a long boring story short, the voice produced from this screen within half an hour, was talking back to me in my own voice. It had seemed to piece together sections of what I was saying in a stuttering fashion where the pieces became longer until they were one sound and at one stage I thought I heard something like Chaucer or old English speaking while it was getting to my level of English. I was by this time, asking questions. It said that it had prior knowledge of language here but had not been updated recently. So far, I was still fighting with the fact that this could all be done on Earth at the moment. The next seven or so hours I just asked questions and was given answers. At no time did the device ask me anything. I was listening to me so I knew there was no other person here. No green men appeared and I tried to take pictures but everything electronic I had was rendered useless. There is a really convincing explanation for this later because naturally, I asked why my electronic devices were not working! You would ask where it came from as a matter of course and it could only put up big pictures of what looked to me as stars. It said its origin had ceased to exist and because our time is related to our solar system, could not tell me how long ago either. Even if it could, I was still thinking along the lines of a hoax. I wasted a lot of valuable time walking around looking for hidden people or wires leading away and even set off to look for more vehicles and to get an explanation from the range warden.

CHAPTER THREE

3. The Questions.

I asked if the craft had a controller here on Earth. No. Just to cut through about 15 minutes of Q and A the summary was that this craft is identical to the craft sent to each planet in the solar system. It is released from a Mother ship which has come into the solar system on such a trajectory and speed that it stays eclipsed by the sun and is on an opposite orbit to our Earth. Why? So the possibly inhabited planet detected from far out in space does not retaliate or in some cases intelligent planets have automatic asteroid destroying capabilities that do not always distinguish between possible peaceful visitors and rocks! It even went into showing me video of the crafts or probes, as I shall now call it, being spun up and released on a cassette type launcher. The Mother ship is a whole chapter but just to say it was vast and under fully automatic control. This is because as we know from our own space program, signals do not travel fast enough to traverse galaxies quickly enough to control spacecraft. The control section of what can only be described as a computer on the Mother ship is minute in comparison to the database stored on it. The Mother ships computer is a whole new chapter.

After finding out the probe was not attached to the Earth in any way I went back in and asked how this obviously heavy probe was staying off the ground. The answer is long and complicated but this was one reason why I wanted to air this to see if anyone knows what I am talking about when I explain it. In the main body of the probe there are two CONTRA rotating disks. These are as

big as the base and one spins clockwise and one
anti-clockwise. They are held in a magnetic field
and have what seem to be fixed magnets on the
disks and electro magnets on the hull of the
probe. I was told there was a total vacuum in the
chamber where these disks rotate. Thats the easy
bit. Some of the fixed magnets are used by the
Mother ship to start the disks rotating. The
disks are traveling at an insane RPM and fixed
magnets on the lower disk are passed by alternate
pole fixed magnets on the upper disk. This
apparently throws out a terrifically high speed
alternating and strong magnetic field. This
cancels completely any other force or wave in the
area of the disk. It is powerful enough to stop
electrons flowing in wiring and the alternating
magnetic field causes them to stop flowing even
in DC circuits where they are stopped, forced to
move backwards and forwards in an almost AC
fashion and then because of the high frequency
actually stop altogether. This is why all my
electronics failed. They had not actually failed

but had all their electrons in the wiring
stopped! Electronics start working again properly
about half a mile away. Having canceled all
forces around it then it is the same as sitting
still in space. The vast Earth may as well not be
there. So the hum was these two disks spinning at
a very high rate. Due to the high speed, the
sound has gone out of our hearing range so the
disk appeared silent. I was informed I would hear
it if I were on the Mother ship when it wound
down in its dock where I would hear a high
frequency whistle first as it came into my
hearing range.

How do you move through space if you have
stopped everything? All I can say to us
earthlings is to buy a gyroscope. Once it is
spinning and you try to turn it we all know it
shows big resistance. Spin a huge gyroscope and
it is impossible to turn it quickly. Well, if it
was not attached to your hand it would have gone
in the direction of least resistance. The probe

pushes one spinning disk away from the other on one side by tilting it slightly. The probe then will travel in the opposite direction instantly. This is where UFO observers have witnessed skittish behaviour and ultra high acceleration and speed. The magnetic fields are so strong that they can affect light also and the result is a change in the perceived colour of the hull because the field has changed the wavelength slightly apparently changing the colour of light hitting your eye. I understand people witness changes in colour of UFOs when they are about to move. This is where my limited brain left the plot! I was shown complicated diagrams and 3D animations of the inner workings of the disk and although only two moving parts were apparent there was a mass of magnetic influencing areas some having 3 jobs, some two and some were dedicated to one job. There were fixed magnets to hold the disks and some doubled up as opposing magnets for the moving fixed magnets to act upon, some were electro magnets used to tilt the disks for traveling. These took power from the generating coils on the rotating disks. The disks were spun faster when entering a gravitational field and some magnets were used for this also obviously to retain "charge". I was becoming interested now and asked the probe how long it was here for. I had given the probe some idea of time by stating that the Earth did one rotation in 24 of our hours. It knew time but didn't know what our increments were for it. It was then able to calculate hours and minutes and announced it was only here for about 9 hours. Its stored knowledge of time on Earth had us having 400+ days in a year and apparently that was quite a few million years ago. I wanted to know if the fact that we only had 365 days now meant that we were traveling round the sun faster or were we getting closer.

So what was the reason for the visit? It was obviously data gathering and this is complicated too. I will say it all quickly and then go back in detail. The Mother ship senses nearest planets while still in another solar system and decides where to go next. On leaving, it uses all available planets gravitational fields to fling itself towards the next target and then shuts down having charged itself from the light source we call a sun and also from the rotational energy left in the returning disks. The probes are stored until needed in their cassette launcher. Time is not an issue as with humans. Data has been downloaded to the Mother ship and assessed for anything new.

The detailed version is this. There is so much to say here I might get ahead of myself. Our solar system had already been targeted whilst the Mother ship was at a stop somewhere else. Now to answer long awaited questions about whether we had been visited before, the answer is many times and by very different visitors. Almost all visitors were here to gather data as we were and still are not considered important enough to

communicate with although some probes which were
not on the "net" of communicating planets have
broken the general rule. Apart from the data
collections which are a bit like us visiting the
jungle to see if there are any new undiscovered
life forms, there are also visitors intent on
possible mineral collection and threat
possibility neither of which we come into. We are
too small to warrant mineral collection and too
stupid to be a threat. This seems harsh but has
saved us from the automatic mineral collecting
visitors that have ravaged other inhabited
planets ! These only detect the mineral they were
programmed to detect and were made by
civilizations long gone. They come in, send down
mineral collecting apparatus some of which looked
massive and do not know if a planet has life on
it or not ! In other words, it shovels everything
up, places it in the processing plant, makes a
mountain sized pellet and shoots it in the
direction of "home". The worst one of these
evolved some beings which adapted to travel on

the "moon sized" craft. They jump off during the collection process and collect things they want like water and supplies for the next stage of the journey. I was not surprised to hear that humans and anything organic were a potential food. Back to our Mother ship and it is halfway to this solar system where the transmission part of the ship which has been supplied with new data, then transmits it over years as what I now know to possibly be Neutrino bursts. They are weeks apart and are in two types, long and short, or zero and one and are in a universal language known to around 250 advanced civilizations that know each other and are on the same "net". See chapter on The Information System. A quick one on civilizations. After the big bang which did happen but isn't the biggest, it is a medium sized bang in our area, and happens after all matter has been reduced to the smallest particle or wave. An anomaly causes the reaction and I was shown what happens but may not be able to articulate it in words as it was a diagram I was looking at, and all starts flying outward and combining into more and more complicated molecules. We know this already. These get far more sophisticated until in exactly the right conditions, molecules combine into complicated concoctions until we arrive at DNA. Unfortunately for all you religious types out there you have been scammed. The Earth was not made by God in seven days. The reaction took 7 billion years + and it did itself. The system requires no control from outside at all. As the galaxies form some collapse again and explode and all chaos breaks loose. Life forming is quite a big hurdle too. Out of 20 odd million possible life supporting planets there are about 250 more advanced than us, around another 100 known about but not on the "net", 50000 planets containing bacteria with about 100 at the sea life stage. The soup has to be right before you eat it ! The list is long. Right minerals, exact temperature by being the exact distance from your light source to let water flow, become a gas and go solid, protection from your light source i.e. ozone for UV and a strong magnetic field to deflect the harmful stuff which means a metallic core moving in the right manner to create a strong magnetic field. Just to top this, none of this can form whilst water is about as it requires great heat. So then you have to wait until you get hit with an ice based asteroid big enough to give enough water to cool the planet and settle it down enough to form your consomme. Then stuff can sit around for millions of years without anything happening but those with a moon get a method of stirring and as we see ours causes the tides and swishes everything about. The idea is to get as many different molecules in contact with each other as quickly as possible and unlock the right sequence forming the first complicated molecule. So life is rare and in fact there are only about 250 civilizations ahead of us and about 50000 at the cellular life form stage as was said above. We on Earth are slow starters due to having some severe setbacks. Setbacks seem to have been the reason for different development rates and here we have had them all. Volcanoes erupting causing ice ages, being hit by asteroids, massive solar blasts from the sun slows early life, gravity inversions let in solar energy destroying plant life.

By the way, you are African. A catastrophic event (ice age, volcanic eruption) wiped out most plant life and reduced humans to a few 1000 in one area of Africa, We all stem from this one point and still should have the DNA to prove it. All you racists and "I am better than you" merchants should disappear up their own orifices about now. There is no such thing as American, British etc. we are all African. And just to show how we are heading in the wrong direction, the 250 odd civilizations ahead of us do not have a "type". Each individual is allowed anywhere on their planet without being the slightest hint of a problem. A history of this development came from near catastrophic events happening frequently where all beings have dropped all to come together and avert disaster. Whats the point of fighting for your area when impending disasters are going to destroy all of you if you do not pull resources. We are in a relatively remote area of space where nothing really happens but some planets deal with asteroids on a weekly basis! We are fighting over stupid things here but not looking at the bigger picture where we could be destroyed in seconds. Others are fighting to keep out of black holes, most have made Star Wars type "escape" planets which you would call a "Life Star" as opposed to "Death Star" as in Star Wars due to doomed home planet. See Chapter on The Life Star. I was shown a universal design for one of these and was advised to build one as the things that can destroy us number in the 1000s. These "Life Stars" are so common as nearly every planet ahead of us has had or nearly had to use one. After all, we here on Earth put life rafts on our ships. We already know the Sun will eventually engulf us. I was told at the same time when I asked about precious minerals etc. that we were quite rich in the right things to survive and that all gold and precious stones will be required for things other than jewelery! To build a "Life Star" we will need to tap into our metallic core, build manufacturing plants in space, perfect a method of getting items into space without burning anything. This probe was one way and we were advised to acquire this technology as fast as possible. At this point I was shown the probes 3D internal diagrams again in detail which I later realized was the probe showing me how important this was to our survival. A space tether was shown to me and how other planets "in the know" have built them. Just to fill you in, most of the 250 planets receive data from each other via particle burst transmissions. I asked if we could be on the "list" and was quickly told that we would have to get our act together before any long term communication was possible. Why can't we receive the burst transmissions ? We could but the people monitoring space were looking for radio signals where they should be looking for faint rises in neutrino levels and recording how long these are. The phrase "hello" takes the system 9 months to transmit. Why is this? A week long burst of neutrinos may be so broken up after great distances that if it were short or weak then it would probably just be background noise after a short distance. I was told we needed a detector outside our solar system first with relay stations on every planet and preferably a string of detectors and relay stations OUTSIDE the galaxy. Very funny. Not much chance of that happening soon. The system on this probe knew we had sent a probe outside our solar system and that it had taken a long time to get there and I said to the probe that we had called it "Voyager" whereupon I was shown a picture of it which came up on the big screen. It was heavily pitted from "micro meteorites" but the plaque depicting life on Earth was still visible and the probe I was standing in was just an elaborate one of these.

The "plaque" in this probe was replaced with an information screen and data was exchanged enough throughout the universe for it to know quite a bit about us even though it had not been here before.

In the next few chapters I will elaborate on subjects in greater detail. And I will show you why the general information about us flying around the universe at this time is showing us to still be a bunch of savages. But I think we already know this.

CHAPTER FOUR

4. The Country System.

As we see here on Earth, this does not work. You have rich countries where we think about what to buy next and what hobby we could do and what to collect. There are other countries where because the human was born there instead of a rich country, has to see her child die from lack of water. Here in England we waste a gallon brushing our teeth. Then you get the people in rich countries saying he / she was born here so deserve the best and people in poor countries trying to get to the rich countries yet we go to the poor countries on holiday ! Then there are the more sinister actions by big corporations who bribe the leaders of the poor countries to keep taking their resources. The leader is getting so much money they couldn't give two hoots about the people of that country and how poor they are and hungry and then when they rebel they are shot and the leaders rounded up and jailed by an army / police force bought with the rich leaders cash.

No Country system equals no Armies required and The cold war / WW1 / WW2 etc would not happen, a human is free to travel anywhere, resources belonging to the people, if you have to have a government then it can be centralized instead of 180 odd Governments all over the world all singing from different song sheets but stuck on the same globe, no inter country disputes, no customs, all areas become rich together or not at all, no countries based on religion (Gaza / Israel would not happen) you carry on thinking about all the things that would / would not happen while I concentrate on the next chapter.

Also think about the money spent on defence and looking after borders, passports and related documents, customs, putting up asylum seekers and the like. There has been enough money spent on border and defence related stuff to give everyone on the planet a million Dollars therefore not needing to protect ones resources in the first place.

CHAPTER FIVE

5. Employment.

Here on Earth we have got it wrong. The idea is to have everything done so we can sit back and enjoy ourselves. Currently, we get up too early, have a rushed breakfast, get the kids ready to go to school (out into the cold, brave busses, traffic, abduction threats etc., to a nasty building, mixing with kids we want to be friends with but also with ones we don't, get bullied, become a clone of all the other children etc,) then we rush to work all at the same time causing pollution and chaos, get into work and probably do not want to be there, have bosses that push you to breaking point and pay you very little, then the Government steps in and takes a huge chunk of your wages (and then take more when you buy petrol (over 60%), car, insurance, food, clothes and everything else) and you get home tired then argue with the wife and kids because you are all tired and it goes on. You know the routine.

In other worlds, the roof over your head and the food you need are free and a right for you to have it because you were born on that planet and the resources are partly owned by you because of this. Also, on most planets the transport system is free and your buggy comes with the free house. So you can get up when you like, eat (some planets provide the most wholesome foods and the Centres of Excellence provide the luxury food, others are all take away with central eating or delivery.) watch vision related entertainment or listen to sound related entertainment. Then if you go out, your buggy will take you anywhere free.

To go to a Centre of Excellence to pursue a hobby / eat good food etc. you have to provide a service to the planet. So it is a bit like money but each percentage point closer you get to going is relative to the type of centre, how difficult the job is and what is left to do. Here we call this planetary service a job. On most planets a being never stops learning. Here on Earth, we used to stop learning at 18 ish and then go to work. Here on Earth you can now go back to university etc. so we are trying. The problem is with our system one can only learn at the same pace as everyone else or if you are particularly stupid, will hold up the rest of the class. On the mobile device everyone seems to have on other planets which is an elaborate version of our mobile phone and ours are still Stone age by comparison, you can learn anything. So you can do what you like and not be stuck with a course because that was the only one with places left on it. You can also do it at your speed be it 3 weeks or 3 years. As you pass the levels in your chosen course you also up your percentage closer to going to your chosen Centre of Excellence. Once you have passed the course, jobs automatically start coming in to your mobile device, you may find yourself turning up with a seasoned being to guide you through your first jobs and this is inbuilt into the system. You would have had practicals at the Centre of Excellence for that trade also. You do the job then video or photograph it which automatically goes onto the employment part of the system. Once on the system, the person who you did the job for rates you and the work along with anonymous people now unable to do this work who are stuck at home or disabled people who have been in that trade or have shown great knowledge of it. You are then pushed up the percentage to your goal which is going to your Centre of Excellence. The beings I was seeing on the screen that the probe decided were similar to us showed them going on "holiday" sometimes twice a week! I want some of that! This system does away with Pensions (people are able to do something), retirement (no such thing), bad workmanship. Bad job equals no more jobs sent to you. But remember bad jobs are usually down to limited money anyway in this world and this is eliminated with the throwing out of the monetary system. You will not get picked for that job again, or will not be the first to be picked until you go back to the Centre of Excellence and practice. Rip-off workman no longer exist as there is no money to be taken and no rewards if the job is not done and of course, people not being able to afford the work etc. you just log the job on the system and rate it when it is finished, no boss will be pushing you because you are an individual and work for yourself (normally, The Boss has to make money which no longer exists, you are your own boss, no firms to go bust, all the best tools provided by the Centre of Excellence, no paperwork or taxes to pay which seems is the biggest problem here when starting a business, I could go on forever at the muck that is cut out with this system. All beings work alone and for themselves. If there is a job involving several different people then each task is placed on the mobile device of the qualified person. If you were shown to be particularly good at one part of your job and had a high ranking from last jobs, you will get offered that bit.

As the planet gets more perfect there will be less jobs so the system automatically lowers what you have to do to get to your Centre of Excellence. You may only have to do two jobs a week. Planets I was shown where the abodes are underground had obviously no maintenance related to ageing and weather, this is one of the biggest problems on our planet. Something needs doing on the house we have to find the money, get the builder, then as soon as the job is done it starts to deteriorate from day one. The underground house only needs maybe a change of interior colour every now and again. I owned an underground ROC Bunker once at March in Cambridgeshire and went to preserve it but when I got there and opened it there was nothing to do except paint it inside. On the hot days it was cool and on cold days it was cooler but not as cold as outside. A candle burning actually made a difference to the temperature and three candles provided enough heat. In my first experiments there and about the same time as flat screen TVs came onto the market, I set up a camera looking across the fields and fed the signal into the TV and sat there a while at the table and it was just like having a window but without the drop in temperature. With todays 4K ultra HD TVs and matching cameras there would be hardly any difference. The TVs power supply provided enough heat to keep the bunker warm.

Jobs will be higher rated if they are emergencies and need doing fast and also if they have been offered on the system for a while with no takers. All those who have passed first aid would be given a complete kit ready for their job and if someone logs on a medical emergency then all first aiders in that area will get the alert on their mobile device.

CHAPTER SIX

6. Memory.

I am going to go over memory hopefully before the chapter on Death. Lets imagine a wide ice cream cone containing hundreds of layers of ice cream going down to the point at the bottom. The top layer is what we are seeing and doing now. If we move to the bathroom our brains change layers and we go into toilet mode where the memory of how to brush your teeth comes to the top. If you are thinking about something else you usually stop for a second or if you have done that task every day you will carry on in automatic mode but probably will not remember doing it or have vague memories. These memories are changing layers based on everyday life. As you go down the layers there is a degree of compression represented by the cone getting narrower. It is used in computers now where a line of zeros will be replaced by a number representing how many zeros and hence saving space. You can test this by looking at old photos. You remember the family member but look around inside the photo and in my case there was an ornament in the background remembered that I would not have if the picture had not have existed. It is still in the memory but you would have never thought of it again had it not have been for the photo. This will probably trigger a whole series of other memories like what was in the room, your Mother throwing it at your Father and remembering what the argument was about etc. Videos are exceptionally good at triggering. Triggering use to be for us walking great distances and as a landmark came into view you would recognize it as going the right way even though you could have not remembered it before hand and what sequence the landmarks would have come in. I can do this driving across London. I could not tell you my route but just know where to go when I see the trigger landmarks. These trigger memories to jump several layers to the top. We have all developed a great memory for faces derived from having to know who beings are to determine if they are from your settlement or are from outside and a potential threat. These days you know you have seen someone before but do not know where. A bank clerk will be known in the bank but if you happen to meet him in the local supermarket it may not come to you immediately who he is but comes later on. It has been stored in a lower layer because it was not important except when in the bank where it is triggered as being the bank clerk. As you go down the layers you get to a point where sleep is required to remember something. I have been in many situations where something or somebody has been talked about but his name has eluded the conversation. The next day you remember it. Music is good at triggering. You will not remember a track again until it is played whereas you even remember the words and can suddenly sing along.

The bottom tip of our memory "cone" is so compressed it only comes to life in an emergency or life threatening situation. It is our instinct and is so small it can be passed on in the cell produced by a womans ovary that eventually leads to another human. This contains fight or flight information, a lot of automatic things we do when we are born etc. Some animals walk almost immediately etc. Above that are things to do with conscience. If this was not there then we would go around killing people with no remorse or regret or even thinking it was wrong. Crying if something is bothering us is another when we are babies. This alerts the Mother if something is wrong. Above that is everything we have seen or heard in our lives based on importance. There will be some incredibly trivial things your mind has decided you will never need but the automatic system driven by circumstances you are in sifts through the data. To rearrange this vast amount of memories takes the whole brain so is done while we are asleep. Memory sorting done by your visual cortex results in dreams. I asked why we tend not to remember dreams ? If we did our memories would become full in a very short time. It is automatically not remembered as it is derived from the memory system already. I have covered what happens at death but just to remind you, the whole memory evacuating as told by patients who have died on the operating table and have been brought back, results in you seeing your whole life in great detail. Unfortunately, bad things are stored in our deepest memory (because we have to remember if a family member dies from being in a car crash or in ancient times, attacked by a wild animal, this is more important than the memories of your 18th birthday etc.) these memories come to the front and some patients being revived have reported being embarrassed at what they have done as the bad bits fly past. The last second or even smaller amount of time and the last deep memories will seem like an eternity to you and will appear to last forever. The worst deed you did generally comes out after your good memories and will be with you for what seems to you to be an indefinite amount of time but actually you died. Going up the level of importance, your dead relatives may be your most important memory and if you did nothing bad that overshadows their memory, you will think you are with them forever. It is an extreme version of waiting for a kettle to boil. If you rush to the toilet it is finished before you get back but if you stand staring at it it seems unbearably longer. Whether you are with your last memory as bad or as good this has been misinterpreted by religious types as eternal damnation or hell or if you did good, eternal bliss or heaven. The white light people see when they are close to death is your sight system shutting down and is caused by the cones sending their top most signal which is bright dazzling light and the rods which are mainly catching light around the perimeter of your vision, do the opposite. The result is a dark tunnel with a very bright light in the centre. Even this has been interpreted as a God by religious types. People who died on the operating table also report not wanting to come back as it was that good basically because all nerve endings have died and pain you had whether you knew about it or not, ceased!

CHAPTER SEVEN

7. Religion.

You are not going to like this but I could not give a monkeys. Someone has to say it.

Basically, we have all been had. Religion, in any form, is a way of controlling huge numbers of people by using fear. Four or five thousand years ago (a split second by universe standards) religion didn't exist. This was news to me as I had been brought up thinking a single entity created the universe. It is all a load of rubbish. But I still can't knock it as in some religions and parts of the world, it has produced mostly better an more peaceful people by making them think they will go to hell or face death if they do anything wrong. The Jesus and God thing came to my mind as I had this drummed into me from an early age and this caused me to ask about this.

Very few beings have visited Earth as most is done by unmanned automatic probes. After a big bang, all material is moving outward. Galaxies form and are moving away from each other and eventually, the gap becomes too wide and visits become less frequent. Earth was visited lots over its lifetime of a few billion years and the last flurry of activity by visitors was timed for the advent of the thinking human. Up to this point, humans wanted food and to reproduce and didn't think of much more. As they became aware that if they could "move the bushes" to one area and forage without having to walk far they would do this. Planting crops came about. With a concentration of goodies all in one area came the need to protect the crops etc. from other settlements. War was born. Chimpanzees are beginning to attack other groups of Chimpanzees with sticks here now on Earth. One global catastrophe killed most plant life and humans were dying out until they realized they could eat the animals around them even though it was out of desperation. This is why we like a good steak. We were never designed by evolution to eat meat and were foragers eating fruit, nuts and berries. The last place left not ravaged by an Ice age was Ethiopia and surrounding area where you still get thin, tall people. The thinness is caused by the lack of needing energy storage because food was all around them on trees and bushes and the tallness is to be able to reach more food. The rest of us followed the ice back to the poles and were living on animals where there would be one big feast after a kill and nothing again for weeks so we developed fat storage which also doubled as insulation against the cold. We need one big volcanic eruption or asteroid hit to go back to these times which has reduced us to between 400 and 2000 humans left on The Earth.

As we already know, at the point humans had enough food and were content the thoughts go to what is around you. This happens to a certain extent today. Some countries have inhabitants fighting to get enough food and a roof over their head, which takes all their time and thought, whereas other countries have inhabitants who take these things for granted and their thoughts are now elsewhere on their hobbies etc. sipping Champagne and taking in a Theatre Production before eating a £100 gourmet meal in a French restaurant. We worshipped everything at some point. The sun, moon, dogs, water, the weather, volcanoes, fire, holes in the ground, gods of crops, gods of everything etc. or anything unusual.

A change came when a Mother ship was a way outside our solar system and its acquired knowledge using the universally available communication system talked about in this book, it could see that if there was not a course change on this backward inhabited planet we call Earth we would destroy ourselves so the ship set about growing some beings to plan a system to set us on the right course. The ships makers had long gone as they didn't make a "Life star" and their planet was destroyed and the population taken on by another planet. In this case the control system for this Mother ship was on a universally known control protocol and so it could receive instructions from the central net. Three beings were grown over the last 40-50 years it took to reach the earth and because the inhabitants of Earth at this time were not believed to have any knowledge of space, the Mother ship went into orbit around the Earth. A probe almost identical to the one I was standing in took the beings to the surface. The beings had been genetically built to breathe our atmosphere but it was realised it may not convince all as the humans built looked like the last data collected on Earth humans taken when we were almost apes! This would have been right if everything had been left to evolve normally but visitors between then and when this ship arrived attempted genetic modification. So a human woman was impregnated and followed until it gave birth. We know this woman to be Mary and the baby was Jesus and it goes a long way to solving the immaculate conception thing! The Star of David was the Mother ship in orbit making sure Mary came to no harm and the three "kings" were the beings bringing things to make sure the baby had the best start in life. In history, it is a bit of a grey area as to where these Three Kings came from. Now you know. To cut a long story short, the baby grew to be Jesus who we know most certainly existed and we also know he went away for "40 days and 40 nights" where he was shown a screen similar to the one I was looking at and because he was a being of knowledge for that period in time (daft!), took quite a long time to show him how to set mankind on the best course. Once the probe was convinced he knew what to do he was released. The being who appeared to Jesus a few times was a being from the Mother ship and may well of had a beard and white cape (for instance!) so as to hide his ape like features! The beings and the Mother ship were then responsible for the various illusions required to make Jesus look gifted, magic, caring etc. so people would follow. This included doing cataract operations on the blind to look like they had regained their sight. The Mother ship left when it thought things were going well despite having to rescue him a few times etc. These stories being told over and over again became heavily exaggerated! The Mother ship was to return within 1700 to 2000 years and this would be your "judgment day" where the "time machine" program on the main computer in a Mother ship can enter data for each particle present on a target planet and as we all know by the periodic table, there is not really that many and all those can be broken down into Protons, neutrons and electrons, it also knows how each element reacts with one another, again not hard as we have done all this already on Earth, then predict how each element reacts with other particles then can recreate the whole planet as a computer simulation. It is then possible to rewind the simulation from any vantage points on the target planet and see who did what etc. Each being that did something wrong would be punished but didn't say what this punishment was. Genetic modification was talked about. This is what we would probably call the Judgement day where all the nasty stuff is eliminated. If you read the chapter on death you will see the system that has been put in place naturally for us to be "punished" in our own judgment day the seconds before we die. The Mother ship in our case had been reset to deal with planets that had a chance and as we know, the Romans were not very Jesus friendly which made us look like we were not savable, so didn't return to us and the 2000 year mark would have been perfect as this would have stemmed the sudden seriousness of religious intentions from some religions to still want to conquer the world for themselves. It was pointed out that successful nations like England who conquered and formed the Commonwealth, even if it had conquered the world, would have broken up eventually anyway. The Roman Empire failed and quite a few others too and in fact, none of them survived. All Empires ever built anywhere in the universe have failed. The same with religions. Heres the theory. If you were to convince every person on the Earth to join your club and they all did and had no problems with it, you actually arrive at the same point where all beings are their own bosses anyway. Even the name of your Empire will fade because there is no other Empire there for you to have to use the name to differentiate between Empires! The Catholics are on a downward spiral with their Paedophilia and the Muslims are on the up and, I am told by the probe, will take over for a brief spell murdering all (if we do not challenge it) those who do not convert but will destroy themselves from within due to infighting. If we survive this and all other things we cannot control, you eventually get to the same place that most of the other advanced planets have arrived at and that is any inhabitant, being allowed anywhere, with the main identity of being a citizen of their planet, who will say he or she was born in England and NOT "is a citizen" of England. When you try to isolate yourself from others, you become a target. When you gather resources for yourself, you become a bigger target and so on.

The Jesus and God thing did work and to this day produces people who are kind, good hearted, and have the interests of other humans as the most important thing. Just to cover a sensitive issue and I am going to come straight out with this, the probe states that there is no known superior being or a creator or evidence of one on the system and it has been universally known that from the smallest particle at the beginning of time to the best planet with content beings is a well trodden path and the process is no secret with the "chemical reaction" known fully. You do have "superior" beings that can help a developing planet on its way as in our case but these are genetically created by incoming probes / Mother ships and can take any form. We hear of giants, one eyed monsters etc. in mythology. Who knows where these came from.

Unfortunately, some rules that were OK 2000 years ago are not OK now but are still pursued. When I asked which ones I was shocked by the answers. I didn't know young boys still have all the loose skin chopped off their private parts in the name of religion. I assumed it was a medical thing. I asked what the skin was for and it is to facilitate entry during sex so the female internal skin is not pulled. Today, on the Internet, you can find testimonials from women who have had both saying the un-butchered one is better. Of course it is, it has been designed by evolution over millions of years where the designs that didn't work were dropped by nature. I asked how this custom came about and why people would want to do this butchering going against something they think their "God" created ? The custom stems from old men calling themselves Bishops and the like, wanting to become involved in little boys penises. And this is true today. In the Philippines, an un-butchered boy is made fun of. While there is still money around and if you have had your privates butchered then sue the knickers off all those responsible and for every penny. You will purposely have had this done at an early age so you cannot possibly know which version is better and because you will never know the people responsible have robbed you of this choice. Sue the buggers. Apparently, little girls don't get off so lightly in Africa either. They have parts removed normally with a rusty razor blade, no anesthetic either, then cannot ever experience orgasm because "It was to do with the

Devil" etc, and then theres others which have parts sewn up only to be opened the day they have sex whereas it is sewn up again after. It was certainly "Earth bound" rules made up by very twisted "religious" beings many years ago who must have been ruling by fear. "Oh! Hello. I've come to chop the skin off your little boys penis. If you do not let us God will punish you." Not while I'm alive you don't. These practices are what outsiders look at when assessing how far we have to go to get out of our "Savages" phase and its rank in the table of requirements is just behind the limits of the monetary system and the splitting up of a planet into parts which are both considered backward in relation to what is out there.

Some religions say it is OK to throw stones at people who commit adultery. There is something called "Sharia Law" that some people think it is still OK to use even though it is 1000s of years out of date. These people are incredibly backward.

We all love a good wedding but having one life partner is relatively new. Our brains work on patterns and there is a memory section which sorts the good patterns from the bad. A shapely woman is registered in the memory of all men in the good section high up with favourite foods etc. All men usually come to the same conclusion when a group of women are sighted, as to which one is the prettiest. It was there in the instinct section but comes to the front when we are a certain age. If it did not we would not be here. A woman has the responsibility of making sure the man is good for providing food and is strong enough to defend her. So the shape stored in the womans memory under favourable shapes is the fit man with muscles showing driving a good car (has possessions)and living in a good house (somewhere to bring up babies). There is an automatic default here and the following example was shown. If a man and a woman are marooned in a spaceship or in our case, on a desert island they will eventually begin to like each other even if they are not the images they first had of their ideal partner. I can relate to this. I moved to Corfu with my Mother and Grandmother in the 70s. We were on a farm miles from anywhere and had one family as a neighbour. There was a plump completely simple Greek girl who was good at milking the goats but nothing else. After a few months of not seeing any other females, I began to like her. You instinct system is changing you to carry on the species. But back to the subject, humans will dump the marriage bond for quite a few reasons these days and the reasons seem to be becoming petty. The fear of what the church and local people would think of a separation has gone. There is an exception and that is when someone is regarded as what is now known as a soul mate. The method of finding your soul mate is covered in the chapter on happiness and the information system.

Marriage is quite a new thing also. Humans have had life partners as far back as time but this was due to nesscesity. Signing a bit of paper keeping you together and all the stuff that goes with it is very new in relation to how long we have been here. We are held together by factors outside love so if the love goes out of the relationship then the couple have to stay together for lots of other reasons. Children's welfare, do not want to lose the house or other possessions etc. Well, the probe had a solution for this too. Unfortunately, all other things talked about here have to be in place first.

Just to show you how people can still have their God, Tibetan Monks in solitary prayer, due to the power of the human brain, can create a "friend" who, although not visible, can take any form you like in their mind, say whatever the creator likes and do things the creator wants to see. Try it yourself. I have a blue eyed blond 6 foot Viking female sitting next to me and the

first thing she did was remove all her clothes.
Tibetan Monks also report these mind created
friends can also turn nasty. If you tell
interesting stories of a great being when all sat
together in the right setting (a Church) you will
become a follower of this being and, like the
created friend thing, have him watch over you in
your mind. If he is portrayed to be good and the
penalties for being bad are told also, you will
not do anything wrong. This is how a group of
people can create their "God". It can exist in
your mind or the minds of like minded people but
there isn't a bloke with a white beard sitting on
a cloud which is probably why nobody else can see
him.

The mention of a Judgment Day has a certain
truth in it. The day you die and your last
seconds of life is a seriously complicated time
so look at the chapter on death for that. The
second is the planetary information system, on
deciding that things have become too messed up on

a watched planet that could still have a chance, will deploy a task force made up of suitable nearby ships. The target planet has to be worth saving and at the time I was talking to the probe, we were not. The ships in this task force, on their journey to the target planet, would have been sent the data collected on that planet which would have been run forward as a simulation to come to the conclusion where it had become necessary to intervene and would arrive at the right time. It would take control and while doing so, will realign the simulation to what has actually happened on that planet. If it is still needing help, the go-ahead will be given. Each thinking being on the planet will be interviewed and told their good deeds and bad a bit like at the point of death. All beings will be told about what their dead relatives did, good or bad, even back to the beginnings of the thinking being. If a bad deed was done to another person, both will be told and so on. This is not rigid as different planets require different systems. At the end of the "interview" process, those who were sufficiently bad will be punished. The planets simulation is so detailed it can be run forwards so can inform the system if a person is going to do anything wrong in the future.

Theres an interesting fact that when a system is as far advanced as this, no violence is required. The beings on a target planet can be totally controlled in a huge number of ways from being completely incapacitated to types of chemical changes to the instinct system. I asked what would happen if we needed help. For a start, this planet is not considered here to be on a course to ever even get to the stage where we require help anyway which was a bit worrying.

The Mother ship would arrive and gather all Inhabitants in various ways and each would be shown their lives so far and significant acts from their ancestors. They would all be shown how they arrived at the position they were in and if

the bad deed was down to them they would be
punished.I did not go into the punishments but
they were adequate so as not to allow the being
to commit any other bad deeds.

I had a ten minute wait for information on
what to do to improve our chances of getting to a
Judgement Day (scientific version) and beyond. I
was told it is possible to completely bypass the
Judgement day process. The probe was sending and
receiving vast amounts of information from the
Mother ship parked behind the sun. Because it was
not in direct line of sight, it was using other
probes that had been sent to other planets in our
solar system to relay the information. This was
all by particle burst transmissions but luckily,
a much faster version than the interplanetary
transmitter. See chapter on the information
system. Heres what came back :

If you are going to have a "religion" it
must be based on your fellow planet inhabitant

and not how to control him. Controlling Religions, especially by fear, are called a Cult here. Your religion is your planet. This is your "God". It's what keeps you alive and allows you to live. Your "Devil" is anything bad that gets in the way of this goal. Full stop. If you have two religions there will be trouble at some point. Only believe in what you see. Do not listen to anyone else and certainly do not follow rules made up 2000 years ago to appease a twisted mind from that era. What is good is pretty obvious and you do not need a preacher to tell you.

From birth to maturity, the inhabitant should only be exposed to learning about the following :

Most important. How to react with and treat another inhabitant. This includes actual interaction and secondary interaction where it is all inhabitants duty to make sure all planetary needs are fulfilled. i.e. if there is a shortage of a foodstuff then you go and help in that area. Your goal should be to leave every inhabitant you meet in a better mood, situation etc. than when you arrived. Whether you like it or not, your instinct as a human on this planet at this time, makes you feel good about yourself every time you do this. We are much more inclined to help out if all our own needs are complete i.e. Food, abode, transport, entertainment and a partner. We are so far down the slippery slope of money and greed and selfishness that we have not been considered as survivors in the universe. I am not a Bible basher but I seem to remember Jesus disappearing for "40 days and 40 nights". This is how long it took to teach a normal carpenters son of the time (extremely simple) what is happening on planets far advanced from us that have made it and are likely to survive indefinitely. He "rose into the heavens" (pulled up by the probe there at the time) "God showed him the way" (the image on the screen in the probe was one that looked like a being of importance at the time). I asked if this image was in the memory and was instantly shown a bloke with a beard in a dress.

In the learning process deals with Earthly things first. Maths, History and all the rubbish we don't really need was not there. Maths in advanced planets just is not required as the planets systems take care of any mathematical stuff. These are considered pastimes and if you are interested in these subjects later on in life then you learn about them as a leisure activity. You need to be able to count obviously in order to ask for 3 or 4 of a food item and if you are a scientist you would have had the maths course best fitting to your field.

Forcing your religion on your offspring is OUT. They may choose to study it later in life as a history based hobby but only if they want it, not when or if YOU the parent want. You should be teaching them to interact with all other humans and not be forcing them to join with groups of people who think other similar groups are inferior or even as in the cases recently, should all be killed. In an advanced society, especially one without money, nobody is forced to do ANYTHING. Chopping bits off your children is a savagery considered by watchers to have put us back 1000s of years. Tradition is not an excuse. Read about it in future years, yes, a bit like blood letting in past centuries and witch hunts etc.

One thing the probe was able to calculate was what the famous figures in the world of religion would think of the situation now ? The Jesus's and Mohammed's and Deciple's etc were all jumping up and down, pulling their hair out shouting, "This is not what I meant, this is not what was supposed to happen!". God did not have a simulation because he was basically a computer simulation based on a very important person of the time Jesus saw it as mentioned above. Allah was a fabricated "being" also to be used to control by fear. "Allah will get you if you don't act like I want you to!" etc. But as was said before, a big group of Muslims thinking of Allah as their hero / icon can create him as a "friend" in their individual minds, as used by the Tibetan Monks, and he will become very real and possibly the image you have created will appear at your point of death but it still will not be a real person meeting you as such but just the image you have stored like persons at death that see their relatives. You will see the relative / person that is deepest and has the biggest "presence" in your mind at the time.

#

CHAPTER EIGHT

8. Money.

Money is classed as a big problem. Those who have none want it and those who have it want more. All planets in existence ahead of us do not have a monetary system. For us to get ahead much faster it has to be dumped. The country system of breaking up the Earth adds to the problem ten fold. We can all see this acted out on our TV screens every day where one child is draped in gold jewelery and another is living in a mud hole

with no food usually caused by a richer country
that has stolen all the poorer countries
resources.

Take any being from any of the 250 or so
planets ahead of us and they will tell you they
can go anywhere they like on their planet, eat
anything they want and if they see something out
of place they go out of their way to fix it
instantly. The probe surprisingly told me this
happens here on Earth ! Unfortunately, us Humans
do not have this intelligence. Only in a bee
hive, a termite mound and an ants nest etc. have
the inhabitants worked it out ! We are too stupid
to realize and learn from it. If an intruder
enters a bee hive it is instantly thrown out by
all bees near it. If a hole is made in the hive
the bees instantly fill it. They do not expect
extra honey because they know they can have it
any time they like.

The first step is to do away with anything

tangible like notes and coin and make it all electronic. The reason governments do not do this now may not surprise you. Backhanders. There is too much money to be made, even with people in office, that misses the taxation system that they will not dump a cash system where they can get extra money off the radar. Everyone is on the fiddle in some way or other.Corruption is everywhere but some are just better at hiding it. So, everything is now on a universal credit card. Because there is only one system if cash leaves one account it can be seen entering another on the system. If anyone pinches anything or commits a fraud then it is instantly flagged up and even a fine extracted at that same second. This also allows the system to go fully automatic and no human will know anything about anyone unless they do something that requires further investigation.

After the whole planet is on a single "points" server. This can be a real computer or processed by unused memory space and time on all beings personal devices. Using all personal devices means that if some data is destroyed, it is still saved many times over on the "cloud" created by the system using free space or allocated space on all devices, so all data is safe. A being who works for the planet for a set time then is "paid" with time at the centre specializing in the leisure things he/she wants to do. Computerized devices have redundant processor time and in some cases, 99% is unused mostly. Spreading a system throughout the personal device system makes any big building full of hardware redundant. If the data is fiddled with somewhere on the system it will not match all the other stored files that were identical so get eliminated instantly. It will be impossible to add points to your score without it being flagged up. A policeman will not knock on the door and no crime agency or any other human for that matter will know as a fine is instantly taken if you try to fiddle.

Example. You wake up in the morning and your job is a roofer for instance. You have passed all the courses in that subject and jobs will automatically appear on your system. You check your personal device for jobs you have become qualified for and see a tile has come loose on a roof a few miles from you. You click the job to show it is being dealt with and go straight there and fix it. Using the personal device or a video unit attached to your helmet / clothing you would have recorded your job. You then let the owner know it has been done and the owner quickly looks at the photos / video and passes it. It also gets passed by fully independent people or many persons around the planet on the "Internet". This allows less agile people and housebound beings that were qualified for those jobs in the past, to still have a job. This equals NO RETIREMENT. As long as the person can still see and move a finger he / she can still be an assessor. After these jobs are done and the roofer has reached his full percentage to go away for the "weekend" he can then choose where he wants to go. Centres of Excellence are used for leisure time in most planets. This allows the best of the best to be available to any visiting being. At this moment, if you have a hobby, it is limited by money, things you have collected are not stored properly, go into disrepair, there is no money to fix them, they get destroyed by fire or flood etc. A Centre of Excellence has all the best of the subject, stored properly with experts running the centre. These centres have accommodation and food laid on. If you show particular interest or appear many times you can become more involved etc. On a planet I was shown where this has been the norm for about 5000+ years, a type of vehicle used on tracks like our roads was collected in a Centre of Excellence after the whole planets transport system went underground, and the centre has a vast area of old tracks made the same way as in the past with real period buildings etc. and the visitor can drive these, learn the history, work on them and have an experience only a rich person on this planet and time could afford. An example on this planet would be when, and I say when and not if, our transport system goes underground, a person liking Ferrari's can go to the Centre of Excellence for Ferrari's and have the full experience. Most people in our system would not be able to even afford one in their lifetime. No money means there will not be a cheaper option for anything. The best item will always be built and available. So the builder will be using all the best items and therefore do the best job therefore the chances of needing that job done again is improbable.

The dumping of the monetary system which limits us considerably, will do away with banks, robbery, mugging, hunger, and all the obvious things like Governments ripping us off, the need to save to get things done which wastes time, redundancy of having cheap and expensive versions of everything, does away with the need to "Box shift" to keep up a companies existence, I could carry on forever.

A money free planet does not waste time and effort manufacturing inferior goods because the best materials are available for the best possible version. That version has a complete recycling ability because there is only one type therefore no huge cost breaking it up and that is if you even have to. Dyson Hoovers are a good example. These are completely modular and you can buy any part new or second hand and in theory, keep these Hoovers running forever. This is halfway to the goal. Soon we will not have the materials to carry on as we are as most of it will be corroded or half rotted in land fill sites as that which is not FINANCIALLY VIABLY recyclable in our world and is dumped. At some point in the future we will be digging it all up again anyway. It is possible to build a car that lasts forever but no company will build one because as soon as all individuals had a car they would not sell any. A great amount of effort and time has been wasted making one companies car last slightly longer than a rivals. The governments will allow degradable products like this because they would not get the taxes in if everyone had items that lasted.

The planets richest 1% own 40% of our planets wealth. That is a ridiculous figure and why beings die needlessly on a daily basis. The probe says we should stop burning oil as this will be needed for lubrication jobs in the future. In fact we should not burn anything. We are going to need all of it.

A rich country will never be safe from those that see the difference in living standards and their beings will pay by not being safe elsewhere on the planet. They will be a prisoner in their own land.

At the moment, the chances of this money free system being implemented is low because the Toffs need this control so they can have most of the money. They will say that jobs will be lost etc. Think of the amount of jobs related to the monetary system. All these people will become available to carry out research and implementation of the money free system.

All will have a mobile device allocated to them, all will have free accommodation, food and transport. All will have free media like music, T.V. etc. If you want to do your favourite leisure activity all you have to do is complete jobs on the job system to get your weekends away.

Because there is no money, it will be most peoples choice to eat out or get take aways delivered. Central cooking saves a massive amount of energy. But if your leisure activity is cooking then you can keep the kitchen and have weekends away learning to cook and earn the next weekends leisure cooking for the masses. It all works. The stress is removed, things get done much faster, medical waiting lists become nonexistent, nobody has to save to have something done or get something and I could be here all week listing these benefits. I was shown about twenty different planets where this system has improved almost overnight, the lot of the entire inhabitants of these planets. If you want an example here look at small villages where there is no money. All jobs get done.

Lets just quickly go through some of the things that will be eliminated if we went to this system which is followed by all known planets more advanced than us :

No money worries and obviously, no debt.

No stealing.

No drug dealing.

No corruption.

No MPs lining their own pockets.

No immigration.

No adverts on T.V.

No class system. Everyone will be equal.

No Toff schools. Equal learning opportunities for all.

No Insurance.

No phone scamming or cold calling.

No waiting until you can afford something.

No budget or inferior products.

No Chinese imports.

No death waiting for operations.

No pension problems for providers or receivers.

No Social Security system.

No death due to cold weather.

No ripoff banks trying to control the Government.

No gold reserves which can go to the electronics industry.

No cost controlled recycling.

No money driven anything wasting resources.

No pushy salesmen.

No jobs done with inferior materials.

No jobs done badly or to a time limit.

The new system works as follows :

When you become of age you can choose where to live. Space is no longer a problem because all abodes will be underground, with optimal sized rooms. You choose your decor and layout which gets installed before you arrive. The people involved in the building, making the wall panels, painting, electronics manufacture have all been rewarded with coming a percentage closer to booking their next stay at their favourite subject Centre of Excellence. You are allocated your own buggy for the transport system. You can then go to your abode with all the usual stuff like house warming parties etc. again done by people qualified and wishing to further themselves to their next stay away. From this point you can change walls for different colours, layouts etc, have furniture changed, flooring, lights and these are all interchangeable in seconds by removing the whole wall panel. You may have already earned a qualification and when you register for jobs in your area they will appear on your device. If you wish to do the job on that day you will put your name on it and go and do it. If you do not move from your abode your device will de-register you and place the job back on the system. BUT you will then be known to turn down jobs and so may not get important time sensitive jobs come up on your device in the future. Once the job is done, it will be assessed by the owner, people on the system who have the qualifications but can no longer work and anyone else in that subject registered to assess jobs. These assessors also become a percentage closer to going to their favoured Centre of Excellence. When all are satisfied with your job you get your percentage. The incentive to get all jobs done soonest is that if there are suddenly no jobs to do in your area, ALL get to automatically go to their Centres of Excellence. As we have seen in the Employment Chapter, you are then assessed and are allocated a percentage advancement towards your next stay away. When all jobs are complete,

with the best materials and to such a high
standard that the job never needs doing again,
there is then the possibility of the reverse
happening : MOST days are spent doing what you
want to do and only a few hours work. You do not
loose out if there are no jobs.

CHAPTER NINE

9. Information System.

The day you are born and while still all in the room with witnesses, you will have a DNA code created. This is loaded into a new portable device and given to your Mother and Father if present. Like the red book in England for babies, all that is done to you medically will go onto this device. The number created by your DNA maybe a mile long and you will not be expected to remember it. It will be part of a series of security measures when you change abodes, get food, acquire items for your abode etc. It is obviously everything else too :

It will have a screen for video calls and entertainment like T.V. and games here on Earth.

It will instantly come up on your home big screens whenever you walk in the room.

It will have your entire medical history and learning stored on it.

It will register all your possessions as you acquire or change them throughout life.

It will show you all that needs to be done in your area that you have become qualified to do.

It will show how close you are to booking your next stay in a Centre of Excellence.

These are some of the things I picked out most relevant to this planet.

Other planets use a similar device across the board and some beings have had a chip implanted that communicates with the mobile device and the very advanced have had the whole system built into their bodies !

Heres some other uses that may be good for us from planets that have a Male and Female of the species :

When a being reaches a certain age their device allows them to access a planet wide "Dating site". See Dating chapter where I will probably repeat myself a bit. This will have all the eligible singles on it. Here we would have members of the opposite sex and maybe other genders like Gay, one night stand etc. On other planets there is 10 to 15 different genders. Male, Female, same sex female, same sex male. Then there is what relationship you want : One visit, marriage for life, holiday partner etc. One that stuck out was the "Honeymoon" section. This is where you can fall in love and have a honeymoon period for however long it lasts! Then there is the types of sex listings. So on a

planet with 6 Billion beings there will exist an
exact match for everyone. Watch what you pick as
a subject because when you have had some
experiences as for instance a one night stander
this will all be recorded and will appear on a
future dating history download to another
possible partner who might not want someone
"used" so a "Does Not Matter" box will have to be
ticked.

The other important factor here is that your
life history is on the device and although it
will not send the actual data to anyone else it
will say how close you are to being similar using
leisure and educational data, if you buy the same
items meaning your shared abode will be good for
both of you, your food preferences and your
hobbies / Places of Excellence you have visited.
This should get the final compatibility figure
down a bit and hopefully find an exact match.
Exact matches are unlikely to separate and
therefore no marriage certificate will be needed

although the marriage should be celebrated and reception party should be big when you both agree to stay together. After all, we are here for fun and all other stuff gets in the way.

The main system will also be on everyones device. The processing power of 6 Billion devices used in parallel is terrific and probably many times more powerful than any supercomputer of today. The processing power will be used on your device when you are not using it i.e. when you are asleep. Also, the total database of video, photo and music can also be stored if a small amount of memory is allocated off each device and the backup of personal data from all the people on the planet. This means that if your device ceases to function or gets destroyed then your new one will gather all the data from the storage "cloud" based on other peoples devices.

NOW ! One reason why I am spilling the

beans on my encounter is because things keep being invented that this probe told me about fifteen years ago. I have just mentioned "storage cloud". I knew about this on the day I saw the probe and actually thought that other planets had created a magnetic cloud that floated with all the other clouds and held data sent there from our computers for a small fee. Now I know that this is a hard disk somewhere on a server that stores data for you so that if your computer goes pear shaped you still have the photos etc. On the day I heard about storage clouds here I suddenly realised what the probe was on about. Also at the time, mobile phones were used for phoning people and slowly they have been becoming like the devices I had seen on the big screen. I was shown a more or less human shaped being arriving at his / her abode which incidentally was just below ground and on entering the first room, a screen came to life with all the things to do. There was information about food, sound, vision and scenes. The scenes put a picture of your choice on the screen and looked like a window. Here this could be a moving scene of New York from any window there, footage from a camera anywhere, or just outside your house from any direction. Here on Earth a flat screen TV is now less money than a double glazed window. I can't remember thinking the house was underground after the point where the being entered. There was a door with a buggy interior also and you stepped into the buggy closing both doors behind you, entered where you wanted to go on your device and it would automatically feed itself into the transport system and at what seemed like a very short time, the being was where he / she wanted to go !

CHAPTER TEN

10. Abodes.

Where a being lives is a big part of their life and sets the stability of that individual, and when one does not have to worry about the place you live, allows the being to look further afield at what he / she wants to do etc. The roof over ones head should be free and every persons right. Here, we struggle to buy our house, struggle to furnish it and normally our tastes change halfway through obtaining everything for one room, nothing is good about not being able to buy a house and then not being able to make it how you like it instantly. I was shown planets with lots of room and planets with a space problem. The one with lots of room had what they call an ideal climate. All weather had ceased as there was no outside influences, the planet was in an orbit like the moon where there was a dark side and a light side and which didn't rotate causing differences in temperature. Days as we know them didn't exist. Beings didn't have a nation as such and could wander anywhere, the abode system went underground 30000 odd of our years ago because solar radiation was deemed to speed up the deterioration of the beings bodies etc. If you wanted another room you just placed the need on your personal device and unmanned machines turned up which were controlled by people on their devices, sitting at home, anywhere on the planet, who were qualified and specified for that job and appear within a very short space of time and worked non stop to complete it. Their transport system was underground, travelled at high speed using magnetic levitation in a tube with coils individually powered by solar. These are modular so one can be replaced in seconds. Every being has a buggy which is inert with no moving parts except the door. The personal device tells the coil and junction system where the buggies occupier wants to go and because the "vehicle" has no being controlling it, can travel at maximum speed all the time. The beings on a planet I was shown live in a band at 90 degrees to their sun because the part nearest the sun is too hot and the bit in the dark is too cold. The band has an area bigger than all the planets in our solar system put together. A smaller planet which had a radiation problem early on due apparently to a weak magnetic field, went for the "glass" dome option with abodes in layers going down into the planet like colossal blocks of flats in reverse. This system too has a perfect temperature control as heat is taken from the bottom of the building deep in the planets crust and transferred around the structure. The structures are linked again via buggies running in tubes. It took the probe and I a while to calculate speed but between us we think the fastest these buggies could travel was between 1000 and 2000 kph between structures which were a long way apart. Travel time was not even enough to read a newspaper on this planet.

When a being arrives home, the personal device can be put on any surface which will charge the device wire free. When I was talking to this probe wire free charging didn't exist and I remember thinking that this could not be possible. It has become reality as I write this. The device also puts up any communication etc on the big screen of the room you are in. There was a screen in every room and the data and sound follow you. When the screen is not working with data or vision then a scene (moving) of the inhabitants choice would be on. The rooms you were not in were devoid of light and all screens are off. The lack of a T.V., DVD, computer, clock, gaming console, pictures etc were evident as the personal device was now powerful enough to do all these at maximum resolution matching the beings eyes. If a being prepared foodstuffs at home, heres the method :

You look at completed dishes on a screen or on your personal device, click on the dish and time you want it. The finished food or produce arrives at your abode either by buggy or someone who selected that job because they were going that way or other reason. Being arrives home and prepares. The food producer, the delivery person will all be closer to their next trip to a Centre of Excellence. Jobs that are unpopular get a higher percentage. The recipe was displayed on the "kitchen" monitor and any of the worlds recipes that ever existed, past and present, are on the system.

It appears there are around 100 different food containers on this planet all made of tough materials, that get sent back and cleaned and filled again. They have an inbuilt passive "chip" which can be filled with the data of what is in it, when it was made, by who, its history and the like. There is no such thing as waste on this particular planet and no real evidence of waste on all the others ahead of us. The beings even genetically modified out hair in the wrong place, any sweat related excretions and one planet with the same toilet system as us, made their excretions smell nice. Their waste was 100% recycled with no dumping etc. All waste is used to grow non-edible vegetation and not edible plants so everything is at least two stages away in the food chain.

Heres a list of advantages for underground abodes :

Very little change in temperature compared to the surface :
We can no longer heat / cool our homes as this creates gasses that do not leave the Earth.

No maintenance required on the outside of the house :

Concrete at your set level stays dry and at the same temperature as surrounding rocks.

Surface can be reclaimed by nature :

The footprint of buildings will have to be put back to greenery in order to re-balance the air.

Very easy security :

No chance of someone breaking into a window.

No noise emitted :

Very little noise can be transmitted to the surface or to neighbouring abodes.

Protection from solar radiation :

Solar radiation has already become worse and will be increasing as the sun cools.

Atmosphere totally controllable so no bugs or viruses :

It does not matter what is happening outside as you are in a controlled environment.

A level can be found for your optimal living

temperature so no heating :

The deeper you go the warmer it gets.

Weather never a problem :

Does not matter how hard it rains or blows, tornadoes, hurricanes, nothing can touch you.

Disadvantages are :

Building it in the first place :

This is not a problem with the machines I have seen. See below …

No windows :

T.V.s will replace windows with anything or scene you like on them. See below …

The devices I saw for this consisted of a "digger" which was rolled up, took a room sized square chunk of ground and left again without leaving any mess. Then a room sized mould was dropped in and filled with thermal "cement" with a waterproofing agent sprayed in first and that was about it. Cost is not a factor because there is no such thing as money. I just have to add about the roof of an underground house. The roof came as a prefabricated unit and had solar radiation absorbing abilities but only because they needed it on this particular planet. According to the probe, we too are suffering from solar radiation and apparently, as our sun gets older it will increase. Living underground and having protected buildings puts the beings in much less contact with solar radiation. Some heavy particles traveling at high speed can "shoot" DNA causing malfunctions. Smaller particles can travel right through a planet without touching anything due to the fact that your average atom is only 2% actual matter (even this is debatable) and the other 98% is wasted space. This is what makes it possible to compress a great amount of matter from a vast area of space by a black hole into a core only a few miles across. You had better read the other sections on how known planets have escaped being drawn into black holes. The point of no return is a lot further from the black hole than you would think. Our Galaxy is in fact matter being attracted by a black hole. The Life Star is the only way out.

No view will be another problem with an underground abode.

With 4k 55 inch LED screens available on Earth, just think what is possible elsewhere.

The screens in the abodes were capable of putting any video feed of your choice, from anywhere on the planet, up on the screen automatically when you were not using it and only when you were in the room. This could even be pictures or video of relatives. On a more simple level, a 4k camera outside facing anywhere you want, can put that feed onto your screens.

An underground house could possibly bury you

!

Not with the walls I saw. They were developed over 1000s of years, thermal, liquid proof etc.

Although there were structures going deep into some planets, the normal abode only has to be about 3 feet underground to meet with all the requirements for heat loss and comfort. In fact the roof I saw had a layer of what looked like a metallic shield probably to stop heavy particles traveling in from space. So the concrete, metallic and earth layers would keep anything out.

Some planets inhabitants had been living underground for years due to attacks from neighbouring planets.

A diagram shown to me of an underground community seemed to be an upside down pyramid made of abodes buried in a "V" shaped hole with the "V" being at 45 degrees. This was so there was no great pressure of surrounding earth on any of the walls. I must mention the lift system on this particular community. It seemed similar to our own and consisted of a shaft with a car but differed at ground level. There was a track going away from the top of the lift shaft and roughly the same length matching the depth of the shaft. This track was pivoted at the shaft end so could be leveled so the lift cars weight would cause it to lower itself to the bottom of the shaft and then tilted back slightly so the counterweight would run downhill pulling the car back up. Very little power would be used raising and lowering the far end of the track instead of powering on continuously to bring the car back to the top. Remember, every abode has a transport tunnel ending with your personal transport buggy anyway so the lift was only used for recreational things on the surface. The track was in its own tunnel just under the surface which had been returned to greenery.

Underground, there are places and rock formations on Earth that are so huge they could house the entire world population with gaps between big enough to absorb any sound. No noisy neighbours, natural heating ... I could go on about this for hours. planets which have taken this option due to being attacked either by other planets inhabitants, automatic mining spaceships or meteorites, have acted like a termites nest where as if there were anything to do or needed to expand, every being mucked in. New abode, just dig it. They do not sit there waiting to be paid. There are so few jobs to do in some of these established populations that even the smallest job gets you a place at your Centre of Excellence and sometimes for the Earth equivalent of weeks ! Can you imagine doing a bit of gardening for someone here and your mobile rings to let you know you are now entitled to three weeks at a Centre of Excellence of your choice for instance The Centre of Excellence for the 24 hour party.

Now, because your abode is underground the temperature is constant. If the underground community is deep there will be a system collecting heat from below and distributing it evenly throughout the community. There is no issue with space because underground area is limitless. There is 100 miles of solid stuff before it becomes liquid. Even if we went down a mile we would find this too far. With these two problems fixed you can have big rooms. In most planets and optimal size has been reached. Big enough to move freely and not so small as to become claustrophobic. Because of this the wall panels you originally chose can be taken to your next place if you move. The panels also contain the screens for your media so these go too and in a short space of time. Just say your interest is Egyptian History you can move to Egypt taking the lining of your abode with you. You just apply for a different location on your personal device to which you may be allocated something immediately, log your removal job on the device, helpers turn up and take down the walls, pack furniture etc. and you are off. Once you have been allocated an abode that is it. It is yours until the day you want to move. Nobody can remove you from your registered abode for any reason. If you get old, log the care and medical jobs on your personal device and the helpers will come. They can't pinch stuff from you or rip you off because there is no money, personal possessions are registered with you and are not worth money. If a person dies all registered items are de-registered and returned to their Centre of Excellence and if anything was acquired illegally these automatically reset to their Centre of Excellence anyway and the persons who originally had it and the person who pinched it will be flagged up. If the original owner was still alive it would be returned to them. There will be no point pinching something anyway. If you want something you can apply to have it delivered. Change your ornaments weekly or not at all !

The walls you created for your abode can also be changed at will. You do not repaint you order a different colour / system / storage / furniture and it gets delivered. This includes floors, ceiling, kitchen, bathroom and the like.

Not enough abodes available ? Dig more. A point about digging here. This can be done by a person sitting at home provided his / her eyes are good and they can move a finger. The diggers are driven by people on mobile devices utilising their abodes big screen set on 3D, anywhere in the world. The job is logged, you may get 20 people register or 400 or 4000. Some may operate the digger for 10 minutes but because there are so many operators the machine can run until the job is done. They all play a part and their percentage goes up for their next trip. All people operate the digger. The most accurate digger "drivers" will probably be the majority and this will create the most accurate dig and increase their percentage chance of going to their Centre of Excellence the next time. This prevents idiots going mad with the controls and destroying stuff. Diggers do not look like anything we have. They cut out a perfect room size block in one dig and place it in a similar sized "truck". This goes off to be processed. Interestingly, nothing goes to waste so "Fly Tipping" is a thing of the past. The Earth / rock is sorted into its minerals etc. Artifacts from bygone eras are collected and processed in archaeology Centres of Excellence and it is known where these came from as the block of soil had a grid reference allocated to it. The block going to the recycling centre is reduced one layer at a time so all archaeological data is preserved and items found are logged including position, orientation etc. Rocks are either broken up into usable sizes or returned to the area with the sifted earth to form landscapes over the new abodes. Even grass will be replanted as it is known that to get it to that stage it would have taken valuable energy, minerals and water from the soil. Builders do not actually go on site here. All work is done by machine and by people sitting at home. You could have 120,000 people from all around the world operating 6 machines !

CHAPTER ELEVEN

11. Government.

In the U.K. people become Members of Parliament and it seems any Tom, Dick or Harry can get in providing he / she has friends in high places, paid enough in backhanders, went to a school for Toffs ruling out any "commoner" who couldn't afford a place at the school, has the gift of the gab bluffing his way to the top and of course, stepping on other humans to get to where he / she wants to be. THEN on the train into Westminster on the first day they have real thoughts about how they are going to change their constituency's fortunes which is immediately quashed by red tape, not being able to get a word in edge ways, told to stop "rocking the boat" and develop their own business life before the next election. M.P.s are usually well known people and being human will always help ones self first. This is a basic human instinct. This is why with a money system, they seem to have feathered their own nests. Expenses : Free breakfasts, lunches and dinners, a subsidized bar with their own brand whiskey, chauffeur driven Jaguars, security, cash for questions, a fee for turning up in Parliament even if they are only there for 10 minutes, money thrown at them for election campaigns which is usually by party donations which normally have an underlying sinister agenda. The voter sees a bit of paper every five years with the names of the party candidates for that area to which they put a cross on one and secretly put it in a box. This is purely to make us think we have a say and keep us quiet and pretend we have a free system where everyone is involved. After wasting millions on campaigns and spending a lot of time working on them and not on what they are there for, they then do not do what they promised. Votes wasted. Then they turn around and wonder why nobody turns out to vote. In the 250 odd planets ahead of us, they all seem to have arrived at the same system. The Planet in most cases is run entirely by normal beings and as will be said below, YOU can join a section of Government on your portable device by passing exams in that subject to which your device then gives you the option to join, you start by watching peoples conversations and vote good ideas forwards. If a person has a series of good ideas and gains enough points, they move up a level. You might have 20000 inhabitants qualified on the subject and if 1% is active then thats 200 people running one subject. If the idea gets to the top level of qualified beings and they all agree then a change is made to the law. I will probably repeat myself below because this is important.

Government in all 250 odd advanced planets

is administered by the people. You do not have a separate building with old men shouting at one another. Government is broken up into sections or subjects relating to your planet. Housing, leisure etc. Beings join the subject they feel strongly about or think they can help with, or used to work in. To do this you have to be voted in by beings already on that subject and that is after studying the subject and taking exams. This is all done from the beings personal device from anywhere on their planet. Once inside your subject you can talk about problems and suggest fixes. As you gain knowledge and respect, you move up until you become a member of the front line of "MPs" who are allowed to adjust the law on the central system. Remember, most laws are to do with money, land, travel, behaviour etc. so most of this will be gone. Beings outside your subject cannot vote. This stops people who know nothing about a subject voting for a different reason. The being involved in a section is known by a user name allocated each day. This is important so that other people on the system do not know who you are and cannot befriend you and form "gangs" so there is no link to who the being actually is in real life. In this world it would stop friends voting you in even though you are probably useless at that subject. It prevents "old boy network" and "Harrow types" being voted in just because they went to Harrow School or are a Mason etc. Also, in general conversation on the Government subject site, the conversation does not have something identifiable next to the sentence so the daily allocated "user name" is a must. The sentence saying the right thing or is an obvious fix for the problem is moved forwards to the next level where it is checked and put forwards again by the next highest people. After you have had a good track record the system automatically moves you up. You suddenly get a mail saying you are now at level 20 etc. a bit like a game in this world. You can only possibly be voted into your subject on merit. The voting process inside the subject is fluid and any member can change his or her vote or votes for someone else going up the ladder on the spot and at any time. Voting is totally anonymous. The more votes or backers you have the nearer you get to becoming a front line member able to tweak the law when all agree it should be changed. In our world, the fluid voting or backing system would defeat vote rigging, prevent having to wait 5 years to change a rogue government, stop them spending huge amounts of money on campaigns etc. and prevent the futile voting for one M.P. from three or four parties knowing nothing will change. Policies and promises are always broken.

The completely stupid and very backward system in the U.K. means everybody who can convince people and have "the gift of the gab" can become an M.P. even if they do not know anything about politics. They are thrown into an old building and start off thinking they can make a difference. After fast becoming aware that the system is bogged down in red tape and that they cannot make a difference, they then turn to setting themselves up in case they are voted out at the next election. This involves milking the system for every penny they can get, using their status to start a business, get non-executive directorships and do anything that makes money. If they get to the Cabinet, it is very unlikely they will get a post where they know something about the subject and usually mess the whole thing up. Basically, a massively heavy "ship" has been created that whoever takes the wheel, cannot seem to turn or stop it. Break this up into smaller "boats" and the whole lot will not sink together.

In the money free and country free system there is obviously no Treasury, Foreign Office, Home Office, Tax Office, stealing, drug running, being ripped off, money worries, insurance, having to wait for something whilst you save etc. Five of us went on for three hours running off things that we would not need to worry about again. In a few examples of Government departments on other planets I was given, there seems to be an abode dept, an interplanetary relations dept, a research dept etc. But the job system is the central part of production and distribution. If someone in research develops a new portable device, they alert the jobs section that production and distribution beings are needed and the whole planets devices are changed for the new one and the old ones recycled instantly. Because there is no money system you do not get a cheaper version because everyone gets the latest and best possible. If you make a hole in a bees nest, they all stop what they are doing and mass over the hole and get it patched as soon as possible. Bees do not wait for funding.

If things here were free, you would get lots of people hoarding 20 and 30 of everything. A dept for distribution sorted this out and because everything is "bought" using your mobile device and it can say no if you are being greedy but on most planets beings soon realized there was no point obtaining or changing something until it was needed. Whats the point in having a cupboard full of light bulbs when you only have to ask to have one delivered. This cleaned beings abodes up where you no longer required storage for anything.

CHAPTER TWELVE

12. Transport.

I like old methods of transport. Cars,
motorcycles, bikes, trains, busses etc. These are
all good for museums and Centres of Excellence.
The transport system I have seen makes the
following redundant. Cars : Great fun, dangerous,
polluting but you can travel in private and go
practically anywhere. Motorcycles : Even more fun
and even more dangerous. Allow freedom and the
ability to go anywhere. The tarmac takes up
valuable space that should be returned to
greenery. Trains : Take space, are dangerous,
consume vast amounts of power but are great to
ride on as you can read etc and do not have to

control it. Busses : Used by Councils to save
traffic space but spread germs and although you
can do your own thing like read and listen to
music, you are lumped in with everyone else.

The transport system almost solely used by
the big 250 is in narrow tubes underground.
Mostly, the control is from the beings personal
device, the buggies are completely free of moving
parts except the door, great speeds are achieved,
collisions are impossible due to a build up of
compressed air if a buggy comes too close to
another or to a blockage. Some are driven by
compressed air but the most advanced have coils
around the tube powered by a power source charged
by a solar or wind device. These are triggered by
a buggy coming up the tube and the speed
regulated depending on the type of tube you are
in. For example, when you leave home in your car
on Earth, you are traveling slowly and as you
make your way to the motorway you get faster and
faster. The tube system is the same. Slow when

leaving the abode and fast when traveling around the planet. Air travel went as soon as these planets developed the tube system as the speeds achieved in a tube were far greater than in the air and 99.9% safe.

I did ask some questions and were shown diagrams. I asked if the buggies wore out or created friction or rubbed on the tube walls ? They have overcome this on the air powered systems by leaking air on the non-compressed side of the buggy around the seals so the seals ride on compressed air a bit like a hovercraft. Nothing wears out. Speeds are so great that the compressors are only on for seconds on each section of tube. I was shown a valve system and compressor tube where a valve opens to let a buggy through and closes behind it powering the compressor only in that section so there is always maximum compression and only that section of tube is on.

Only the owner and the immediate family are allowed to ride in an abodes buggy as all have one anyway and there is not normally enough time to talk. This stops the spread of disease also. Behind the seat is shopping space that doubles with an insert into a child carrying setup. So if Mum and Dad both have buggies then there is space for two kids. When the kid reaches a certain age it gets its own abode and buggy.

The air powered tubes have a power source at say one mile intervals where there is a valve and a compressor. The compressor sucks air from behind the valve and forces it down the tube in front of the valve. The mobile device has told the power source the buggy is coming and opens the valve and as the buggy passes it closes the valve. At 600 mph the compressor will have only been running for one second. The valves are designed so if there is a power failure the buggy will open the valve as it passes as it seems to be a long thin sheet pivoted at the entry end so it can be pushed open. If there is a buggy following then the compressor will be sucking it up the tube while it is blowing the front one away. The narrower these are the less power and air you need to blow them so they are generally one inhabitant wide with that being in a seated position. As there is no real time for a conversation or discomfort it is deemed not to be a problem.

Underground tube system cuts out lots of problems like weather, walking to your car, driving, worrying about how your car looks, insurance, tax and MOT all gone, nothing to break or go wrong, no paint to scratch or cause pollution when it dries, no rusting, no deterioration, surface can be returned to landscaping, no road signs, no road lighting, no living being or animal can get run over, no oil, tyres, brake fluid, anti-freeze or fuel to worry about or cause us more problems in the future. Again, one can go on forever thinking of things.

This goes for planes, trains and cars, busses etc. Planes are our fastest form of transport at about 600 mph but 2000 mph sounds much better to be and you do not leave the ground.

Further more, your journey time will be nominal as serious speeds can be attained when in a straight line. The old air tube system for sending paperwork around a department store years ago worked on this principle. Shuttles took seconds to get from A to B. A study I heard about measured G force on a bend to be 28G when they tried to use this system for distribution of delicate objects. A human would be smashed if the buggy took a bend with this force acting on it. The "road" system comes in as explained above where the air pressure is set when in an "urban" setting to only subject you to 1g as in a car.

There was a machine shown to me that although there was no size reference points for me to know how big this was but if the guy standing in the picture was the same size as us this was making the machine about 10 feet wide and 50 feet long. It had two long shiny square metallic molds in parallel coming from the back which were the moving molds for two air tubes side by side. The machine moved forwards slowly digging its own trench, another moving vehicle would fill two hoppers I would guess the ingredients for cement and a liquid which was probably water but could have been different. The cement would mix and was extruded into the square trench dug by the machine which would set over the tunnel molds which were slowly being pulled from the cement as the machine went forwards. The machine then covered the new concrete tunnel tubes with earth from the front digging operation. This was an extremely simple version of what was happening. The machine also : Laid what was described to me as fibre optics, laid electricity cables, two different liquid tubes, sifted through the earth for anything useful and artifacts from a different era whereby only sifted earth went over the tunnels and these would be planted by an army of landscapers operating machinery from their own mobile devices whilst sitting at home. Also, contaminated earth from a past time would be picked up and taken away for processing. Another big space on the machine was taken with the equipment to make sure the tubes were in an absolutely straight line. This makes sure the future travelers were not subject to a rough ride.

Once a planet has stabilized its population, built their abodes, linked them all up to the transport system and you have the majority of the tubes in place there is then relatively little to do. The compressors and valve need replacing occasionally and these seem to be done in one go by sliding the whole block sideways consisting of old and new systems whereas the new system is in play instantly and the maintenance is done on the old one in situ. This is then ready for another maintenance switchover or an emergency

switchover. The whole thing can be slid even
further sideways to reveal the tunnels in case of
an emergency recovery. If a compressor fails
before the other one has its maintenance done you
just switch everything off leaving the valve open
which renders the system just another piece of
tunnel.

The examples I was shown seem to be on
planets with a flat surface and one example that
kept coming up was the huge planet talked about
earlier where only the band around the middle was
used for building underground, one side was too
hot and one too cold. This planet had quite a few
air tubes in parallel going right around the
planet and some of the buggies the probe
estimated to be doing three thousand miles per
hour. Here you may have time to ring home and say
"Put the kettle on!". Because of the flatness of
the surface I asked what would be the use of this
machine where we were in Otterburn? Another
machine came into view where it was fed from the

already made tubes and would dig its way right
through any obstacle but appeared slower. Another
strange device I saw already built was the tunnel
joint crossing a fault line in solid rock. The
tunnel would be opened to say double the width
and height and metal tunnel tubes would take the
buggy from one rock face to the other but was
free floating so if the rock moved the tunnel
would still be attached to the two tunnel
entrances perfectly on both sides. Air pressure
was dropped here to slow buggies down because of
a possible change in course as even a centimetre
would jolt you to one side and then back again at
the other end of the metal section.

CHAPTER THIRTEEN

13. Contact with other planets.

This will not happen until we meet certain criteria at which point we will be automatically contacted. In order to be placed in the information stream, a visit will be conducted to teach the detection technology and the "universal" language. Just to add a small note here, at some stage in an answer about something else, humans here on Earth are advised to all speak their native tongue and have a "world language" spoken fluently. This, apparently will save us a lot of time in the future. In order to meet the criteria there are two things civilized planets, and that is all planets in existence that are further advanced than ourselves, must do away with the country system breaking up areas on a planet and all monetary systems. These two things alone virtually stop all conflict between groups of individuals and single beings. The other two are religion and government. All four subjects are responsible for most deaths on a planet so these were covered in great detail in the question and answer sessions. When we have all these sorted out will be the point where we will be given full access to all information. These include methods of survival, dealing with asteroids, our own sun, famine, escaping from the sun when it expands etc. and we will be shown methods that have been used successfully in the past by the planets in the "communication network". The things ISIS are doing to other Humans disgusts us but I am hoping we are not being watched by civilized beings as they will never let us on the "net". This just goes to show what religion does to Humans when left unchecked for too long. ISIS members know deep down that their "God" would have disowned them for even thinking about being nasty to a neighbour let alone killing. They call themselves Islamic. Right, then I am the Queen of England.

CHAPTER FOURTEEN

14. The Life Star.

We have all seen the Death Star in Star Wars
and was amazed when it exploded in full Dolby
surround sound at the cinema. An escape planet
does not have to be that big but does have to
have a method of destroying things approaching
it. The diagram I was shown showed segments that
fitted together and could be moved about almost
like one of those picture puzzles where you move
tracked segments to reform the picture. It must
be possible to bring in outside segments for
repair normally due to being hit by smaller
undetectable meteorites over great periods. Each
segment is sealed and can be coupled to its

neighbour for transfer of atmosphere and power etc. This has to be the case so that a damaged segment can be isolated from all others in case of puncture, fire etc.

Apparently, you can fit the whole Earth population on The Isle of Wight! So the synthetic planet should not have to be that big and coupled to the fact that beings will be living inside and not on the surface makes for a lot more available room. I have also seen an escape system where units were coupled with long access tubes joining them forming a huge "web" where if one bit was hit by something the rest survived. This was in an area of heavy debris flying about.

How do we get everything up into space to build it ? Was my next question. Since we do not have the manufacturing process of further advanced planets and therefore can't yet produce gravity defying vehicles, the next item is the space "lift". Here I was shown diagrams and working structures of literally a lift into space. This is quite simple. The strength comes from what looked similar to carbon fibre "ropes" surrounding the lift "shaft" and around that were big bags of helium shaped like teardrop doughnuts. The hole took the shaft and the strengthening material and the teardrop shape allowed the wind to turn the "doughnut" down wind forming an aerodynamic structure. Each "doughnut" was able to take the weight of the combined structure passing through it and because each section is accounted for in buoyancy the whole thing floats. It is tethered in space for stability, to a "goods in" station where shuttles pick up the stuff. The real working one I saw was loosely put together and was moving about all the time and appeared greasy and resembled a living thing. The gas cells were attached to the strengthening cables which had notches at intervals that the lift used to "climb" up the cables. Apparently, this was the simplest one and I had no idea afterwards when thinking about it, what the atmosphere was made of therefore this system may not be possible in our turbulent atmosphere.

Another version of this lift system had round gas bags with cups on the outside causing them to spin like a weather vane. This reduced drag and powered the lifts manually or by generating electricity for their motors.

Since nobody knows about this system yet I am calling it The Petersen Lift !

Just to add a small note here. Very few planets known for mastering DNA have developed machines which can design a living being to do any job and their units are installed in many Mother ships from other planets and can create a being tailored to any climate or situation. Mother ships having these systems have been known to start populations on uninhabited planets and the result is to bring them forwards by a few million years. One was successful in building an organic space tether that grew itself including the hydrogen gas bags like seaweed bladders. This grew from a seed and headed skywards! Jack and the Beanstalk comes to mind and when he climbed it, met the visiting beings from another planet which he must have interpreted as giants probably because they were bigger than him at least and the story misrepresented the Mother Ship they were on in space as the Giants castle! The beings in this case had just been collecting samples as we do when we land on the moon.

When traveling through space one has many things to worry about even though they will not bother you for 1000s of years, you have to be ready. Theres scientists on Earth looking for "dark matter". They know it is out there due to mathematic calculations that come to the conclusion that what we can see is only part of it. We only see things in space that emit light. The stuff that does not is out there but not big enough to reflect light from something thats burning. Most of this is microscopic and here we would call it dust. Traveling thorough space at any great speed you are going to run into things. Sub-atomically, running into radiation will damage other atoms and even set off a nuclear explosion when the atom turns from one element to another. Bigger dust will "sandblast" the craft and if you remember me saying the inside of the probe was smooth and the hull was slightly rough ? That was this problem. Even traveling within a solar system just from the Mother ship to a planet will put a few more microscopic dents or holes in the hull. Mother ships tend to be long and thin with a hard nosecone which can be remelted, recycled, layers of it dumped and totally replaced in seconds. It could be reversed and travel backwards as there was a spare on the back end. On a bigger scale we can look at the moon and see its history of things running into it recorded forever as craters. We have a few on Earth too and if you Google this it will show you. Bigger items coming towards you can be detected a long way off but you cannot rely on light as a warning and must use other methods. Black objects traveling in the dark will surprise you. These can be intercepted with the right sized device to just nudge it off course. It is not good to have to steer around it as this uses huge resources if you are on a big ship. So your Life Star has to have a way of replacing lost material which means bringing the segments of your ship into a maintenance bay. You can have everything we have on Earth and the few Life Stars in operation were created by beings requiring far more things to do and space to do them in, than we will want. In the middle was the very first space stations created by the planet and they were in a huge void in the centre of the Life Star. Around this was all the main surface features recreated from their now destroyed planet. Then the units or segments were arranged in a globe around this space. These were joined by rails that they could be slid on to move them about and more rails at 90 degrees to move them in and out to the surface. You could leave it as it is or place another safety membrane over the whole globe and then top that off with a mile or so of rock. This would collect any stray meteorites and even take bigger impacts. It all depends how much time you have and many have been wiped out because they have left it too late.

CHAPTER FIFTEEN

15. Back to Basics.

There is one globe which is where you live
and you are a single human living there. These
are the parameters other planets work by. As soon
as you join a group you open yourself to all
kinds of problems. Here we are in our Country
group, our town group, our road group, our music
group etc. You should be your own boss and
different from anyone else. You own your own
Abode and buggy in most planets and work for
yourself. Because most planets in the 250 above
us are almost perfect there is not much to do and
the percentage points system has lowered the
requirement to such a point that one little task

gets you massive amounts of Centre of Excellence time. What is messing this planet up is the country system creates war, different religions create war, natural disasters do serious damage because all the buildings are above ground and this then takes resources to rectify. This will not get done because 90% of the planets inhabitants are fighting to get enough food let alone beautify their areas around their abodes. The rules are one globe which has to be stabilized and made so we all want to be here so immediately remove yourself from the country, religious, money and joining anything "active" in trying to create an illusion of you looking better than others. You may be better but keep it to yourself and use it to get other humans to your level. If you are better then you do not need me to tell you to pass this "betterness" on to others. They will not then find reason to kill you later on or will at least subject you to ridicule when they pass you and become better than you! You take the jobs you want off your

device and do them so you can do what you want to
do not what someone else wants you to. A planet
with a monetary system is doomed. The only thing
to break this and to suddenly go into a system
like I am talking about is when there is an
impending disaster. A particular planet I was
shown had tried to deflect an asteroid heading
directly towards them. They had managed to put it
off course to avoid a direct hit but calculated
there would be a side swipe putting billions of
tons of dust into the atmosphere for the
equivalent of decades here. Money and country and
any differences went out the window and all
created underground centres full of food and
things to do equivalent to what was on the
surface. This was quite deep but since this was
broadcast on the "net" most planets have gone
underground. All they do now is close the
hatches. The planets on the "net" have also
mapped all potential rocks flying about in space
and have run their destinations forwards and have
corrected their trajectories or collected them

for minerals and building materials. In the past, these would have been hit with nuclear blasts but it was found that the bits could not then be tracked fast enough and could also wipe out valuable Mother ships so collection is the answer. Our asteroid belt is a disaster waiting to happen also. One rock knocked off course could start a chain reaction where nothing could be tracked quickly enough to save us. This is a small part of why the probe was suggesting we should not still be here which was one reason for the visit.

A few examples. By Back to Basics I will pretend our globe is only a mile across and there are two people living on it.

Half the globe is corn fields and the other half is desert with one tree standing on it. One inhabitant has grabbed the land with the cornfields and the other is stuck with the tree. Because the two inhabitants do not trust each

other one gives the other fruit from his tree and
the other gives corn. All works well. This would
work just as well if they were allowed to walk
anywhere and only took food when they were
hungry. But due to the mistrust this is not
happening. If they did trust each other they
could cut the trading bit and both work towards
making sure each other had the foodstuffs they
need. The trading bit is cut out and both humans
are now free to go all over the planet. Wastage
is canceled because before, one inhabitant was
cutting corn to what he thought the other
inhabitant would want and the other was picking
fruit to what the other person wanted. Produce
that was not eaten was wasted. The new system
made sure that only required food was picked at
the time it was needed.

Both inhabitants had to fashion something to
stop the other inhabitant attacking so they used
up resources making weapons in case of war and
put them on the alert all the time so they could

not enjoy themselves.

The other thing associated with the tree was that it produced oxygen for the globe keeping the two inhabitants alive. In the country scenario, the owner has the right to do what he wants with the tree and could cut the tree down. This would kill the two inhabitants and the corn. If you saw him cutting the tree down and you knew it was the only thing producing your oxygen, what would you do? I would go and stop him. Here on Earth we are watching but do nothing. The country where the trees are growing can do what they like with them as they are "theirs". On a global level they would not be allowed.

The Inhabitant owning the half with the corn has a fire burning every night to keep warm as he is on the coolest side. The other Inhabitant is slowly watching the sky turn a strange colour and the air smells bad and his fruit tree looks sick.He reaises this is to do with the fire.

What would you do if you were in his place? I would go and stamp out his fire. Here on Earth we see what is happening but do nothing. On a global level we all work together to see that nothing is burned. What should happen is the cold inhabitant, if he were allowed anywhere would move to the warm side and build his abode hopefully being helped by the other inhabitant or build underground using the heat from his own planet.

Both inhabitants do not want to give up their land as their forefathers fought for it and many inhabitants died saving their plot. We are now a lot cleverer and educated than we were then and globalization is happening even if we do not want it. The Human still has the survival instinct of wanting what they have not got. What happened in many other world cases was that borders, if they were not taken down over night, gradually faded anyway. The border was still there in history and inhabitants still said they were born in a particular area but stopped saying they were for instance "English" but just said they were born in the area of England but were a global citizen.

I'm going to run through some of the many events that have shaped some successful planets :

Catastrophic event. We have all seen the films of various catastrophic world events and I can tell you these would have happened somewhere in our universe. If the population was of a similar intelligence as humans are now and there were say 1000 inhabitants that survived, they would evolve from a survival unit into an African Village situation where everyone had settled into a routine of chores that if they were not done, would upset the entire system. Those that became bigger and split into groups tended to evolve back to something we see now. Money to trade with each other, wars, areas destroying things important to the planet, arguments, tyrants invading other areas, one area not liking what another believes in etc. Those that stuck together and helped each other and thought of another inhabitant as an equal survived and became great. Here, Humans are split into lots of levels decided by Money, colour, belief, size and the like. When a catastrophic event occurs and in most planets where this has happened, has led to one small area or underground complex where a small pocket of 1000 ish people have lived, these 1000 are now totally reliant on one another. All the levels or differences go out the window as survival is now a priority.

I had evidence even though I did not ask the question directly, that Leonardo De Vinci, Hitler, Jesus and quite a large number of well known people were in a situation where they obtained information from an external source be it a probe, a deliberate intervention, information exchange etc. Leonardo De Vinci spent his time looking into the future at technology,

Hitler learnt about how other planets came to survive for a long time. And came up with his "1000 year Reich" and worryingly, one of the most successful methods on other planets to unify a population is to kill all and only leave the people you want. A bit like ISIS wants to do and if a human turns rogue or into an "non-believer" then kill them. Once you have not killed anyone for 100 years then theres a chance the remaining population slowly forget and become peaceful. You then have to live with what you have done. The numbers are not good. Out of the 250 or so planets on the "net" over 200 went through this process. Very few planets have survived that were in a similar state as we are in now which was another nail in the coffin for not being classed by those on the "net" as important. I asked a lot of questions about the other 50 or so planets and how they survived particularly the ones that had remained stable for 10000 years or more equivalent time. On our current course we will not survive.

Heres how to do it. Scrap borders, money, religion and let go of the past. There is a place for all these scrapped items in our history Centres of Excellence. The Centre of Excellence for Money will have a huge museum containing everything on the planet that was to do with money. An Example : The day we say we do not need the Monetary system and on a Friday night, the City of London closes at 5 pm and the whole City of London Banking area will be preserved exactly as it was at 5pm that Friday night. Open areas will have displays of Money related items from all over the world and be cleaned and maintained by people who want to go to their own Centre of Excellence they have chosen for their next weekend away or because that is their interest and they want to stay there. Surrounding hotels will also be preserved and take in visitors interested in the history of money whom can come on their own Centre of Excellence visit when they have reached a level doing things that need doing. Remember, in this world if you do nothing you do not get to go to Centres of Excellence but can do everything else free. You can walk anywhere, ride your buggy or bike anywhere, get basic food meaning not great food from French restaurants or Food Centres of Excellence and the like but from "supermarkets", put your feet up and listen to any device based media. You will not be crucified for being lazy as the current Govt. in the U.K. likes to portray you. When you feel like going to a Centre of Excellence for your interest all you need to do is log on to your job section on your device, pick a job for the day and go and do it. Simple as that. Only jobs relating to your qualifications will be offered on your personal device. Borders is a mind over matter issue. We have been told for many years to be proud of our country and to keep the population safe and keep our mineral deposits and monetary interests protected etc. This is all breaking down anyway with the European Union. Then we can travel anywhere, globalization will occur whether we like it or not. Most companies in the U.K. belong to someone from abroad or most of their shares are owned by foreigners. Most countries have huge populations of different nationalities and religions. If we do not sort this out we are in for one bloodbath after another. The Human should now say, and that is you reading this, and sorry for repeating this over again but the importance is huge, they were born in a particular area but are a citizen of the Globe, World, Earth or whatever you want to call this ball of matter we are sitting on. Secondly, we now know religions were put in place to terrify the population into following someones rules. If this was not an Earth bound individual it was somebody made up by an earth bound individual or a space derived mission but all mainly with good intentions. I have a "get out" clause for all those who think there are Gods of one sort or another and this is explained in the Religion chapter.

Letting go of the past is difficult but also should be recorded in great detail. Centres of Excellence for every single battle ever fought should come into existence with those people showing the highest interest running them. We should visit these and remember the people who died. If a "Judgment Day" Mother ship arrives and we are placed on the planetary "net" we will know all about each battle. Where people fell, what actually happened, decisive moments, what they were saying to each other, everything will be revealed and in the museum should also be what we thought happened here on Earth. It is OK having the absolute truth but not let go of how we thought the battle went also. Memorials will be built for the dead in these centres. Borders should be just a line on a map separating areas known with different names. Be proud to be from that area if you like but do not think you are better than someone from a different area. And if it is shown that you are really better then it is your duty to bring these people in the "inferior" area up to your level and not sit there like a fat idiot pointing.

CHAPTER SIXTEEN

16. Getting what you want.

At present you go out to work, earn money, buy your favourite items, take them home and use them. For 99% of the population, these items are usually inferior due to cost and break or only last a while where you have to go and get another. The Government relies on this turnover for tax money. If you bought a toaster that lasted forever this would not be good for business and the Government would not get revenue coming in and the toaster factory would shut. In the current period, items are designed with great precision to fail just after the guarantee runs out. Cars have holes in the chassis to "let the water out". We all now know it is to let the water in so as to rust it from inside out so we only notice this when it is too late. The car industry was failing a while ago and so the Government created the MOT "to save people dying from defects resulting in accidents". More like to make more cars "unroadworthy" so as to sell more cars. Japan stepped in and destroyed the car industry anyway undercutting our prices by paying their workers next to nothing.

I picked a planet that resembled what we might look like in a few thousand years provided we do not destroy ourselves meantime, and this is how things work : You grow up, learn from your mobile device and growing beings only get what they want after passing that section in their learning program which is all based on their portable device. See chapter on Education. Once you have passed exams in the subject you have chosen, your device will start giving you the things that need doing in your area. These will have been put on the system by other beings i.e. Water leak at such an address. All the people qualified to fix water leaks get the job starting with the closest and go around and fix it. Photos are taken and even video of the fix which are then put on the system. They are then rated by the person who posted the job and anyone else qualified as a leak fixer i.e. a bed ridden or old being. The person fixing the leak gets a percentage closer to going away to their chosen Centre of Excellence as do all the people who rated the job.

We are born, live our lives and then die. On some planets, conditions have been so well tweaked that the beings are almost immortal and in some cases have genetically engineered out failure.

We are only really the keepers of our possessions for the time we are alive. Very rarely are these things kept in "Museum" conditions. A Centre of Excellence will have the whole collection available to see, the whole history of that collection etc. At your house, it could be destroyed by any number of means, stolen, accidental breakage etc. You yourself worry about all these things while you are not at home but if they were in a Centre of Excellence there is no worry. The next time you are entitled to go to a Centre of Excellence you will be able to interact with all the best items and learn about them properly. If you have shown you are capable of looking after your particular hobby item then you can take a whole collection home whereas if you were still in this system of money you would never have been able to afford it.

Heres some of the Centres of Excellence I would like to go to and would certainly leave all my stuff to if it were to be seen by other people and kept in tip top condition :

The Centre for VW vehicles before 1980.

The Centre for the Supermarine Spitfire Mk 16.

The Battle of Britain Centre.

The Centre for Mosquito operations during WWII.

The French Cooking centre.

The Centre for The Vinyl Record.

The Centre for the Mosquito Aircraft Blueprints and Building techniques.

The Centre for Fast Food (Mc Ds).

The Centre for The British Government from 1959 to 1970. Maybe more than one Centre.

The Centre for SAS History and Techniques from WWII to Iranian Embassy.

The Centre for The Austin Mini Cooper Mk 1.

The Centre for The Parachute Regiment.

The Centre for D Day.

The Centre for 80s Disco.

If I was so passionate about any of these subjects and passed entrance exams in them then it would be possible to apply to live there and look after / demonstrate these items myself.

I would also be entitled to still go away at weekends to favourite food centres etc.

Naturally, if you were to show you could look after old collections then you could run a workshop from your abode. Because there is no money, these things would be worth nothing so are very unlikely to be stolen. So fire / water damage is the only things you would have to worry about.

Today, here on this Earth, we would take a lot of weaning off the possessions obsession. A rich man with his Ferrari says that it is his, he paid for it and he can do whatever he pleases with it even if it means setting fire to it. All those with no money never get close to anything to do with a Ferrari. In other worlds, the materials gathered to make it already belong to the planets occupants in equal measures even before its left the ground. Theres no Country system so you do not have countries claiming the right to minerals, there is no corporation owning the land or the rights to mine or rights to the iron itself. The mining job would have appeared on beings mobile devices, they could do the course to mine if they wanted to earn their next stay in a Centre of Excellence, register the job, turn up, mine the iron and quickly become closer to days away for leisure. They are not bothered where the iron goes next. The transport jobs come in and get done, the smelting jobs get done, The Ferrari Centre of Excellence gets the finished iron / steel etc. and repairs / builds new cars. These are then driven on a road system (probably kept from a previous period) or test track by persons having their leisure time at The Ferrari Centre of Excellence. If you show you can maintain, know the history of, drive accordingly etc a Ferrari then the Centre will give you one to race / drive at weekends. Remember, roads will probably no longer exist due to the transport system going underground and the need to return big areas of planetary surface to CO_2 absorbing / oxygen production. So The Ferrari Centre of Excellence will be the only place to go where there will be a road system and a track preserved for you to drive on. If I were creating this world, I would keep all existing race tracks and a few towns just to drive in and make these Driving or Racing Centres of Excellence.

So, the system and only system working for 1000s of years on other planets is if you do something for the planet then you are rewarded. Because you are provided with your abode, transport, mobile device and food, the only thing you have to earn is your weekends / days away at your chosen Centre of Excellence. You are not penalized for doing nothing.

CHAPTER SEVENTEEN

17. Happiness their way.

Happiness on the Earth is when you have enough money to cover everything and go on holiday once a year. Also, having healthy children and seeing they have a good life ahead of them. Only a small percentage of the Earths population are content or have anything like this.

So, naturally, I asked what was the best way for an Earth dweller to be completely content ? There was a ten minute wait while the probe requested and received data from the Mother Ship. It had obtained data on the closest match to our

planet and a small amount of data from another
relating to pastimes.

Temperature plays a part. Here, if we could
set the temperature to 23 C all would be
comfortable. This can only happen in a controlled
environment like inside our house. It takes
energy to heat something on the planets surface
and even more so when it is minus 15 C outside.
An underground house only changes in temperature
by about 2 C between summer and winter, does not
emit light so will not announce human existence
to all in space. See the chapter on Abodes. It is
an eyeopener. It CAN have windows, it will not
fall down, you can reclaim the whole footprint at
ground level and plant it back to how it was a
few thousand years back, you will not be subject
to bombardment by solar radiation (which is going
to get worse), the abodes will be ready to have
their own climate when ours fails, will match the
underground transport system which also relieves
surface space to return to green areas. But the

energy saving is the thing that will just save us.

Food is the next thing. Good food that is right for you. The processing industry producing "slurry" should be banned completely. The processing part of food is entirely there to save money. A good example is what we have seen in the press in the past. 100% beef means no part of the cow is wasted. What doesn't look like meat gets turned into sausages etc.

If everything were free we would all go to restaurants three times a day. Do away with the kitchen unless your happiness is cooking. All 250 odd planets ahead of us have eating areas in very different forms. There are very few "beings" that like cooking and the one nearest to our needs has cooking Centres of excellence where a being can go and cook with the best chefs, food, equipment etc. The Centres of Excellence for food there actually feed a high percentage of the population.

In a money free planet, there are no
supermarkets as all go to eating areas of
different types. It is like us going to Mc
Donald's for breakfast, Pizza hut for lunch and a
fine French restaurant for dinner, OR have it all
delivered. Junk food disappeared a long time ago
in most of the planets on the "network". Some
exceptions are still valid on some planets.
Normally, weight has evolved out of these beings
because they get food when they want it but we
here still have the survival mechanism where we
store food for a time when we have none. The
Earth went from having food everywhere growing on
trees and bushes and we developed an appendix to
process plant material which Rabbits and some
other animals still have, then there was a world
event which wiped out most of this and reduced
the population to a few thousand individuals in
the warmest part of Africa where we became
dependent on hunting for meat. The men of the

tribe would go out and kill something maybe once a month so a big feast would be had and that would have to last you. We developed the fat storage system. Beings that have had the same routine eating at set times for 100,000 years lose this.

In our case we need a good partner. The saying that there is someone for everyone out there but where is somewhere? On most of the 250 planets where they have a male and a female in the species, they have adopted the following. When a being is of a certain age their device then allows them to access the "dating" service which is planet wide. A being will only appear on another beings device and vice versa if their criteria is met. Also appearing on the detailed "CV" will be hobbies and lifestyle in great detail as recorded on your device. You will be instantly matched to anyone coming close and in ascending order with exact matches at the top. Can you imagine being matched to 6 billion girls or boys. What is happening on Earth now is you have 100s of dating sites with bad photos or "too good to be true" photos, no real detail, charging a fortune just to write a letter etc. it is one big mess. What then destroys a relationship is finding out their bad habits, having to struggle financially and the rest. Happiness would be finding your soul mate knowing he / she was the "one" on your planet, having a place to live and not owing money which should have been phased out anyway. See Dating chapter.

Health is another good thing. On the 250 worlds ahead of us, there are no health issues. They have genetically engineered out most problems and if there is a problem, the being is taken instantly to a Centre of Excellence for that ailment and is fed into the end door and comes out the other end either dead or fixed. No waiting. The front runners in the planetary hierarchy have engineered out death by genetically engineering all cells to be totally replaceable. To aid this, there is a total barrier against space borne radiation from their "sun" they are orbiting around, there is a total ban on anything emitting a wave like from a radio etc. and there is no underlying micro poisons in any of the food and they only breathe pure gasses. We here on Earth are being poisoned from the day we are born and depending how and what you are exposed to can shorten a humans life. An extreme example is Cancer. It can be set off by any number of things or "switches". You could throw three switches but nothing happens until you throw the fourth. I asked about Cancer and was told it comes when we start to be exposed to raw or concentrated chemicals. Sure enough, from the time I saw this probe to the present, lots of these things have been blamed for causing cancer. Viruses etc are also a problem. The more backward planets originally put germ killing filters on all machinery with a fan or that was moving air. I was shown an air duct into an underground abode. It was a long flat glass tube with an oblong profile laying flat with the largest area facing the "sun" and was mirrored on the bottom facing up. Any living organism in the air passing through this tube died of "sunstroke" and the air bubbled through a collecting agent that held all particles from the air and allowing the pure air to bubble out and into the abode. See Medical Chapter.

Doing things you like. We have to get up, feed ourselves, put on clothes, go to work to earn the means to pay for doing the things we like. This is all wasting the time we could be doing our own thing. On this planet most people are in a job where they would prefer to be doing something else. I was shown an example planet. All power was taken care of and by the looks of it were similar to the power sources we have here. Tidal, sun, wind etc. They had produced power harvesting equipment that lasted forever so there were no replacement wastage. This planet was subject to attacks for thousands of years by neighbouring planets so everything was underground and the surface was used for enjoyment when there was not an attack underway. They sorted this by placing a protection system which would intercept attackers from the other planets in the orbit of their sun. So for about 7000 of our years they had lived in peace. Because of those attacks which used to be steered towards the areas of solar type equipment because the attacker knew thats where the beings would be living, they developed a "tree" which gathered wind and sun power. These were fake but looked just like the trees around them. The "leaves" were shaped so two of them forming a propeller would spin in the wind. Attached to these was a very small generator. Each two leaf and generator set could un-clip and could be replaced in a second. The broken one would go back to the Centre of Excellence and be overhauled but because of the build quality, this was a rare event. There could be thousands of these on an oak sized tree or just a few hundred on a bush.

The leafs surface was also a solar panel. The whole base of the tree or trunk was the power storage area so there were no huge batteries to hide. In the abode being run by this tree I was shown there were no energy guzzling heaters because the abode was underground it needed very little heat to arrive at the perfect temperature. The electrical devices needing power were the beings mobile device which could be placed on ANY surface to recharge and the large vision device like our T.Vs were sent signals by the personal one. Like us having a 60" 8K TV with all the displayed content coming from our smart phone. There were no cooking devices or garment cleaning devices. All this was done centrally. The occupant ate non-cooked items at the start of the day (the equivalent of 37 hours daylight) and at the end of the day but went out to eat for the two other mealtimes. There was an optimum time for these beings to eat which meant they had lost the ability to store fat. The house I was looking at was near the surface and had big periscopes at each "window" giving you a view across the landscape and letting in light and heat. These were closed down at night. Houses deeper down had "windows" made from flat screen TVs and you could put any landscape or picture on these or use them for entertainment again with the content coming from your mobile device.

CHAPTER EIGHTEEN

18. Percentage reward system.

I am again making a generalization of
planets I was shown where their system could work
here. I have been very vague about the method of
how you are rewarded with a visit to your Centre
of Excellence related to your favourite interest.
How quickly you get there and how long you stay
will be directly related to the popularity of the
Centre of Excellence. So if you were to have a
list of possibilities, you will get the green
light for the least popular one first. Do another
service to the planet and you may get a few more
turn up. It is also related to difficulty of the
job, accuracy of the job, how the person who

benefits from the job rates it and what independent assessors rate the job as. Do a bad job and you may not get that type of job come onto your device again. If you agree to a visit then the Centre you have chosen immediately knows you are coming, gets the room ready, knows what you want to eat as you would have probably registered this in your free time, and if you were doing a specific job, gets this ready and lays it out exactly how you left it. The people who have elected to live at the centre will all be qualified experts. So if you were rebuilding an old Harley Davidson Motorcycle this would be ready for you at the Harley Davidson Centre of Excellence.

Retirement is a thing of the past. On this planet we retire for some unknown reason, at an age fixed by a Government who puts the age up when they can't afford to pay you your pension. If you become tired and cannot walk in the new system you can still be an assessor for your qualified subject. Lots of machinery will be run from a persons personal device also. Even giving advice to a stranger who has posted a question on the system will cause you to be assessed by them and increase your percentage. If your answer worked it will also be registered that you are good at this subject and you will be sent more questions. Your expertise will become fluid and naturally head towards and find, your natural abilities.

Retirement here means you suddenly stop work on a set day and after the retirement party either are busier than ever or go into a depression. I have met retired people who didn't know how they ever had time to go to work and others who deteriorated over weeks then died! Some could not survive on their new income and were forced to move. The nursing home is another subject. In our system you get to your home which is normally one room in a complex, fall out with the residents because you are not used to being around people, the owners take all your money, you get minimal and value engineered food and waste away in front of a T.V. watching programmed repeats you have no control over. Relatives forget you then you die. At your funeral, the relatives fight over your money and leftovers.

New system means that you stay at home. If you want to work for holidays / favourite subject Centres of Excellence (holidays are also incorporated in Centres of Excellence so an Ibiza Party Centre of Excellence will hold Clubs from all eras and even be based on the island itself) you can still do so. If you become infirm you can register for help on the device. No money worries as hopefully, money will be long gone.

The percentage towards your goal system could be called money but its value is fluid. It is worth more if the job was difficult but worth less if the Centre of Excellence is popular. In an ideal situation, the Centre will grow if it is popular to accommodate more visitors.

I will translate how this works in our situation. If you go to a nightclub here you go to a pub first because the drinks in the nightclub are too expensive, get merry then go to the nightclub paying a big entrance fee if you get past the bouncers. You then enter a club transformed out of something else like a cinema etc. and drink more and in some cases too much where fights then break out. Police resources are used and then you have to find your way home spending more on taxis etc.

Each nightclub shut before the new system starts will carry their name to their Centre of Excellence. The club itself will be preserved in a state just before customers would have originally entered. The new club will be purpose built and have all the latest equipment. You will check into the clubs hotel and stay there for as long as you like. The club will be open the whole

time and people just come and go as they please.
This will be free as you have already paid for
everything by creating a better planet outside
when you do tasks sent to your mobile device. We
call this a job at the moment. Your device will
monitor your alcohol intake and keep you in the
"merry" state for your body type and recent food
intake. Someone suggested that the old club could
be taken down and rebuilt in the new centre but I
think the whole town should be preserved and
maintained as its own Centre of Excellence for
future humans to go to and marvel at. London will
become a vast Centre of Excellence where people
can go and experience what life was like in the
2020s. Highlights will be how in the old days,
people filled their transport with volatile fuels
gassing themselves, were restricted by "money"
causing buildings to go into disrepair and then
if they were lucky enough to be repaired, would
be with cost effective inferior materials, shops
sold items in packaging that would then be burnt
or placed in big holes in the ground, humans

would attack other humans to get their money and rip other humans off and pinch their possessions to sell for money. I shall leave you to carry on for a few hours rattling off all the things we used to do.

Here in the west we like to earn money and go shopping and some would say not to change this. These are the people who CAN do this. Most in the world can't even afford their food.

CHAPTER NINETEEN

19. My brain scan.

Things come to me all the time and I have added items to this manuscript for about a year now so instead of waiting for this to reduce I will put this up for publication as version 1.1 at some stage and add relevant items to make version 1.2 at a later date. I have memory triggers which can be based on anything and suddenly a whole lot of information flows. There is a lot as once I did an interview for an underground UFO channel and was changing the subject many times a minute because I was causing my own triggers and one thing was triggering another lot of information. This is how it happened. I stated that I wished I had brought lots of paper and a pen to write the answers down and was told by the probe that I could opt for a Brain Scan which would fill my spare memory with items of interest to me but could not be guaranteed a result. This is seriously complicated but I could explain it on paper with diagrams. The screen I was watching was not actually pixels like our T.V.s we have now. The screen is made up of honeycomb tubes at atomic level that can fire anything. For the job it was doing showing me things in probably the highest resolution 3D I would ever see for a long time, it was actually tracking my movements and setting off the receptors in the back of my eyeballs by firing the appropriate photon to precisely the right position. This appeared as the right coloured dot on the screen. Similarly, behind me was another wall made of the same accelerator tubes. If the corresponding tube on the other wall fired the same particle they would meet and the demo I was given was a small flash in mid air. Timing the ejection of these particles could make them collide anywhere it wanted. Smaller particles could be fired that would go straight through you without touching anything as they were incredibly small and could pass through a working atom without causing any harm. Even if it did hit one or two items in the atom it should not make much difference. I was told that the computer, given time to exchange data with the Mother ship, could fill my memory with stuff that it thinks might be of interest. It did this by scanning the brain, finding out where every memory cell was, eliminating cells that should not be touched and "re-arranging" the polarity / status of memory cells to correspond with the data. I was told that we had lots of memory we did not use but if there was an overrun it could mess me up! I was naturally concerned but was assured I could function correctly but some deep down heavily compressed memory may be overwritten if it was missed in the scan. The side effects would be not remembering some basic functional human traits. I was told the probes window to leave Earth was fast approaching and I was exited to see it go so I opted for the scan. I had to keep still and was told to just put my face sidewards on the wall so my head would not move. A short while later it was done with no feelings whatsoever.

I can remember saying goodbye and jumping off the side but nothing else. I really do not know what happened after this. I "awoke" driving down the A1 and it was like I had just nodded off for a second. I remember being incredibly disappointed at not seeing the probe go. I rang all the people who might have seen me. The Range Warden, the gate house etc. There was food packaging on the passenger seat and it was all the usual things I would buy and the receipt was even in my wallet. It was for a petrol station and had a number. I pulled over at the next services and rang it. He remembered me because of the Jaguar and it was late evening so he had not had many customers. I was asking if I had done anything out of the ordinary and was met with negatives for every question. The only thing I could see as being out of the ordinary was my lack of producing small talk whilst I was paying. He said I did not say anything except thanks. Life was normal from that point on but there were strange changes to how I was running my life. This could have been due to my newly acquired knowledge or something to do with the scan. The first thing I noticed was the two women I was seeing, both unmarried Mothers living in council houses, went out the window and I was looking for my own perfect individual untouched by man and living somewhere in the world. The Internet produced 55000 possibilities. I became extremely picky and wrote to 12. I was soon on the way to meet the chosen few and the rest is history. I seemed to become helpful to people I knew, took an interest in having a family, realized there was more to life than living in my current town and a few other oddities. There were a few bad ones too but will not go into detail here. I can now be asked a question and although I do not know the answer on the day it seems to come to me the next day after a good sleep. I have had no headaches since either and suddenly started needing glasses for the computer etc. The memory system was covered in the chapter on memory.

CHAPTER TWENTY

20. Death.

Do you hear over and over again, people who die on the operating table and are then brought back to life sometimes tell of seeing themselves laying on the operating table and near death experiences involve seeing your whole life flash before you? I was into this at the time so cleared all this up sharpish with the probe.

In life we do things good and bad and have people close to us die before us and hear about people committing suicide etc. I have the answer to all this now. I will try to put the chapter on Memory before this one so you should already know how your memory works. A human never really thinks about the good things they have done as this should be the normal way of going about ones life. If you do something bad you tend to think about it above the good things and probably more often. So these deeds will be stored in a layer above the good things. On death when your memory is unloading the bad things pass through the conscious part of your brain which as in sleep, uses all available brain processing power including sight areas etc. which is why you see dreams. People dying say they had a being showing them all the things they did wrong and report being embarrassed by it. They then see their loved ones waiting for them.

Just going to explain how time is important here. I think in English. This takes a lot longer than if I didn't know a language at all. It is like a computer running a program in an operating system as opposed to machine code. Because the moment you die is in an automatic mode and allocating brain power to the job in hand everything speeds up. Accidents happen in slow motion because the automatic system cuts in and one of the side effects is taking in more information faster so everything seems to slow down. Remember, we are here because space left us alone long enough and with the right conditions, to grow into what we see here on Earth now. We were not suddenly created by another being. There were attempts to steer us in the right direction and some of these did give us the jump forwards that was needed at the time. But the brain has mainly developed by accident. If it were created by a being then we would have total recall memory, be able to solve mathematical problems instantly, know exactly what to say and when to say it, drive perfectly etc. etc. and the list goes on. We have a conscience. We know or have a gut feeling about whether something is right or wrong. Simplify this into the following. Just say we only lived for one day. You met two people in this time and one you took money from and the other you gave the money to. At the point of death, your conscience is leaving your memory or unloading and the thing you are going to remember is taking the money because this was the memory played back because you thought about this more often and so it was at the forefront of your mind. The mind does not know time so at the last second of death, the thing bugging you most appears strongest and will seem to be forever even though you just died. This appears to be your afterlife. Just for the record in the real world, everything ended there. This explains why a good persons memory ends with them thinking they are in eternal bliss forever and why someone who has killed someone or what appears to be the worst thing to do and that is killing themselves or suicide, well here the memory ends with the subject in what the Bible has misinterpreted as eternal damnation but is in fact the last memory you had that appears to you to be forever even though it was only a second. I will tell you how a person living 2000 odd years ago found out about this later. It is a consequence of the brain becoming sophisticated and is based on the survival instinct. People who die on the operating table and come back report being in a place they do not want to come back from. Even if our conscious mind does not know it, our instinct knows exactly what we like and these are the things that appear in this period. It lasts just seconds but to us will seem like forever. All 250 odd planets on the "network" report nothing after this time. We are really dead. To get over the problems caused by the inhabitants of a planet only living a while will be discussed in this book because I did ask the question. People committing suicide and are revived, come back and report an "eternal pain" even though they were only dead for seconds.

I asked the question about ghosts. Ghosts are what is left if a person dies leaving something they thought was important, undone. At the point of death, the realization that this thing they have not done causes a moment of extreme brain activity which sends out a burst of brain waves. This is strong enough to "record" itself in nearby objects. These could be anything as all items contain something where the north / south alignment can be changed which is how tape recorders record music etc. Old buildings are good at recording things because the stone walls will have elements in them that were aligned to the north south line of the Earth when the rocks solidified from molten or when they were first created. In an example, scientists can tell where the Earths magnetic field was at various dates in history by the alignment of the magnetized particles in rock from that era. The planets in our solar system also have a part to play. We know the moon can attract billions of tons of water here on Earth which causes our tides even though it is far away, well the planets affect us microscopically too. This led to a whole load more questions relating to Horoscopes and the like. Back to death. The person is dying and when the mind gets to the point where it knows it is

not going to survive, the realization of the
undone deed in the persons life causes this burst
of brain energy, this gets recorded in nearby
objects and if the objects are big and good at
recording, this can be picked up by a live human
later on. There are outside influences a year
later that can make the effect stronger which is
why sometimes you get a vision on the anniversary
of someones death and every year after that. Our
ability to pick up on these signals has
diminished because of our busy lives now but
years ago where there was nothing to do and
properties were not full of wiring and mobile
phone and WiFi signals, a person was far more
able to detect. Children tend to be able to feel
these effects because they have an uncluttered
mind. When you see a Ghost it is not actually
there. Your mind has played back the magnetic
effect stored in the nearby objects. This is why
people have reported seeing only the top half of
a body at floor level because when the signal was
recorded, that is where the floor level was

originally. I asked how an exorcism could work and there was only one possible way. If the person performing the Exorcism could produce a brain wave strong enough to record over what was already there. We know about brain waves leaving the head already and some computer company is already marketing a headband that will control the mouse cursor on a computer once you have worked out what to think to get it to move. If this is powerful enough to be picked up by a headband then think what could be produced in the desperate situation where you knew you were dying and had something you must do before you die.

I asked the probe what was the best situation at death ? The reply was obvious. Do only good things and think about your favourite place, people and whatever you like and in your last second alive you should perceive that you are there with those people doing the things you love most and forever. I say forever as the brain, in a period of anguish has no perception of time as it is automatically allocating time to the most important thing. At the last second of death you will remember the most important thing last and it will appear like it is forever. If you do anything bad then this deed will overshadow all other thoughts and at the last second, this will be the thing you remember. A sad example was an old soldier I met at the Normandy 50th anniversary of D-Day. He had memory problems and his historian told me what he had done and that over the years he had told of a certain battle that took place and all the details but the only thing he remembered now was the face of the 17 year old German he shot at point blank range. No amount of veteran hero worship, call up papers giving him the right to kill, people telling him he was fighting for king and country could change this. I fear this is what he will remember at the point of death and will have to look into that face forever. I knew a battle of Britain fighter pilot who's claim to fame was that he shot down one Messerchmitt 109.

He never talked about it and was in a constant own world. His release was playing Jazz on the piano and fixing cars to sell. His landlady told me that if he sat down for more than ten minutes he remembered the day the plane went into the ground. He felt the thump from his own cockpit. If he dozed off he would wake suddenly with a jump and that was the point the whole thing played back again. We know governments are responsible for sending normal humans to kill other normal humans they do not know and the probe has told me of a "fix" that makes sure this does not happen again. See Government chapter.

CHAPTER TWENTY-ONE

21. Education.

It has been calculated that an average child in a school in this era concentrates for about 10 minutes a day. This goes up depending on how good the school is. All that getting up early, driving to school, dodging the bullies, not getting the girl you like and the rest all adds up to a brain full of rubbish. At home, if the learning process means you concentrate for one hour, you have learned six times more than at a current school, saved on exhaust emissions, had another hour in bed, not risked life and limb on our neolithic transport systems and the rest. Most importantly, you have not become a clone. Kids tend to want to be the same either to fit in, there is a craze or a fashion statement that has to be made or they do not want to be ridiculed for not being all of the above.

We are learning from the minute we are born. There exists an optimum time for learning each individual subject. By subject, I do not mean Maths, Physics, geography etc. but human interaction, manners, writing, work based studies for the job you want etc. The mistakes we are making are lumping all kids into one room and trying to teach them using one or two teachers. You never get all 30 odd children sitting bolt upright, silent and glued to their books especially these days where they know they cannot be hit. We were born with the pain thing built in to make sure we did not do dangerous things twice like burning your finger. You now know that item was hot so will not do it again. If it tickled you would keep doing it and ultimately mess up your finger. In the olden days if you did the slightest thing wrong you would be whipped until blood flowed. Lumping pupils together is a cheap way of teaching the masses quickly using one or two human teachers per class. The clever pupils are held up and the daft pupils do the holding.

Once a planet has a system of communication between individuals which includes data then this old school system should be scrapped. It cannot be scrapped in this age because the parents have to go out and get money so are at work. So we have to be at the stage where money has been scrapped also.

Why do we still have schools ?

Citizens all learn the same thing and are effectively cloned. This makes it easy for the Government to control the people.

If kids are away all day, both parents can work so the Government gets more in tax.

On the demise of the monetary system all becomes simple. Kids have a mobile device allocated the day they are born and a code generated from their genes is input on the device while all witnesses are still present. On that device is the life of the person from the first recorded data being the weight of the baby to the treatment it has, inoculations given and in the school system all work and exams passed. The child can start the learning process when they are able and not at any fixed age. Passing one point in the teaching process triggers the giving of something the child wants. It could be anything they want like a toy, time on a gaming machine, sweets etc. This will be the only way they will get this stuff. We do it now. They can have an ice cream if they are good etc. I think I have already talked about human interaction. At the moment, the child has to go to school whether it likes it or not and sit with the same people sometimes for years. You make friends and fall in and out of friendship, argue and the like. You meet people you hate and sometimes this escalates into confrontations later and even murder. It used to be that if you were a rival with someone you would exchange verbally across the street but the two rivals would be smiling and jokes would be accepted. Now you only have to stare at someone for too long for them to come back at 4am and kill you and your family. So, this can be averted with this method. Bullying scars for life and there is no escape, teachers trying to pretend it didn't happen, other kids threatening violence and hitting which seems to go un-punished in schools but is classed as assault in the real world? In most other worlds, interaction with other children is extremely important so has to be strictly controlled as follows : The child meets other children via their device and they meet up in their house with parent / parents present. It may be they want to study together or have the same hobby. The "familiarity breeds contempt" saying comes in here. What normally happens when two kids meet is there is a period

where they value each other. This then runs out
and a period of them being not so friendly. As
this starts to occur they are separated. Then the
listening period starts. If the child is voicing
that they want to see their friend again then
another meeting is arranged. All the while you
are correcting mistakes and teaching manners.
This all only happens when they have learned the
section on their mobile devices about interaction
with other humans. Using this method you cut out
all the wasted time and grow a group of like
minded friends. How to treat strangers is also as
important. In this day and age if you say hello
to a stranger this is classed as madness. The
school thing comes back when they go on field
trips to The Centres of Excellence for the
subject they are on. Another point is that at our
current schools the pupil does one hour of each
subject and may cover several subjects in one
day. Complete mistake. In other worlds, one
subject is completed first. This way complete
concentration is kept and not broken into pieces

over several months. The memory system works on triggers and triggers on the same subject come a lot quicker than trying to align the memory each time you change subjects in one day. Also, some subjects are not required, others are taken up when you get a job requiring the subject. For instance, when someone is going to be a landscape gardener you do not make him or her learn Algebra but do give him a course on geometry. All children should learn their native tongue plus a world universal language. All languages should have their Centre of Excellence so as to keep the history for the future.

The verbal or physical acts by bullies follows the victim and the bully into later life. Bullies have been killed up to 30 years later by their victims mainly because of the ability to find someone now on social websites. Changing from our age old school system to a home school system, this fear culture will be eliminated overnight, the need to be like other pupils will be gone, the need to dress like other pupils including money wasted on uniforms and most of all, swearing will be nipped at source. Swearing is a disease of the mind and those who do it are usually the types who are followers without a mind of their own and like being addicted they cannot stop and have to fill in the spaces in their sentence to make up for the slowness of producing the sentence in the first place. The first thing my daughter said when she came back from the first day at her Secondary School was that everyone seemed to swear including the teachers. If a child concentrates for one hour a day at home this will be the equivalent of two days at their school in the current system and that is biasing heavily towards this system we have. Some say its only 20 minutes. Mum or Dad can stay at home in the new system as the house, transport and food are free.

CHAPTER TWENTY-TWO

22. Food.

We are heading in the right direction. We seem to be eating healthily now but there are still people on the planet not eating. The other planets do this : The food is grown and is usually processed on the spot by people enjoying what they do. There is no Govt taxes, no Council Tax no tax at all. Their abode costs nothing and their food is free. They can really get down and enjoy farming or whatever they produce and keep the business in the family. It will never close because of cash flow problems or the like. Their product is placed in one of the 100 - 200 odd choices of containers and the chip embedded in the container is then loaded with the information. It is taken by themselves or a person qualified to transport foodstuffs to the place of sale and placed by them on the shelves or if it is a luxury item taken to The Centre of Excellence an example being a French Restaurant. They are given their visits to Centres of Excellence of their choice when someone takes their product off the shelf in the "Supermarket". The supermarket will look like the supermarkets we are used to but will also run a menu and distribution service for people wanting delivery. The person wanting food then enters the supermarket, is weighed (this does happen) and the data automatically registers on the mobile device. You can walk around as normal but the chips in the containers send the label that we see on our products now which can be the same colourful labels we have saying "Buy me!" but on the screen of the mobile device. Paper labels will not be available in the future as it will be a valuable resource. Also, menu suggestions will appear with lists of other items you need to complete it. If you were weighed and the device was loaded with information suggesting you need to slim down a bit then items with fattening contents will not appear after a certain amount of calories have been reached. All those in the family will have to be there. The Supermarket will also have cinemas, kids areas, rides, games, other shops and generally be a day out and in other places has helped make sure families get out together more often. Examples I was shown where beings were similar to us showed the centres also having medical areas with scanners, blood and waste testing centres with instant results. I saw lots of examples of dentistry and most appeared to be what I now know as implants. Fifteen years ago these were unheard of to me. There was another method which I didn't cotton on to at the time but I now know this to be tooth regrowth by planting stem cells. There was no such thing as cavities and the only reason for going to the dentist was if you had an accident where teeth were knocked out. No dentures, plates, the need for braces had been eliminated or never existed. Here in a money free society, you would have white fillings until the tooth was no longer fillable and then go straight for single implants as and when needed. Dentists here now on Earth doing five years at dental school working on pigs heads think they will get their revenge by charging the public huge amounts for these "special" treatments when all they have done is price themselves out of the NHS and the public market. So dentures are still with us. Tooth maintenance continues in decline except for the rich.

Here on Earth if we had the choice of how to eat, would go out to restaurants every night ! Delivery and eating out are the norm for most of the planets I saw. The nearest planet to us for how we are mainly changed to the above system but if you took a course on the mobile device and Centre of Excellence you became entitled to install a kitchen and have ingredients deliveries. This would start at how to boil an egg to full wedding cake production or the like. Here on Earth we have a chaotic system where the food industry wastes vast amounts of food and we have people dying of starvation. This was another nail in our coffin for not being allowed onto the planetary network. We are still too savage.

CHAPTER TWENTY-THREE

23. Medical.

Heres a great one to get ones teeth stuck into. UFO or not we are in a right mess. What is happening with our health service here? It is a Dinosaur chained down with corporate types charging massive fees, drug companies pricing much needed drugs out of the market which is indirectly murdering people because of profit, doctors and nurses seem to be running the place by working huge shifts for little pay.

The awful reality is The NHS is the best system in the world. The rest of the world pays. Many pay with their lives. The NHS can be described as a massive 200 mile long Cruise Ship where the engine and the rudder are no longer strong enough to do anything about controlling the ship. Theres about 20 Captains all talking at once and paying themselves ridiculous amounts, there are six million stowaways, the hold is full of counterfeit drugs and equipment made in dodgy countries that pay the workers a bowl of rice a day and produce goods designed to last a short while or fail after the guarantee runs out and the worst thing is the Super bugs are taking over and the legal department is inundated with compensation cases so much so that a whole new industry has emerged with Lawyers asking people if they have been subject to a mistake made by The NHS.

I asked what other places do. Or what we should do meantime. Stop selling things that put people in a position where they have to visit a hospital. The items in this category could be only available at a Centre of Excellence and if

you indulge in them then that gets put on your
mobile device so you do not go there too often.
An example is if you book into The Centre of
Excellence for The Ministry of Sound then what
you drink will be registered and computed by your
mobile device to let you know if you should come
again next week or leave it for a while. No human
will have access to this information unless you
have to go to the Doctor or a Medical Centre of
Excellence.

All the old Hospitals should be preserved as
they were the day they shut so as people
interested in our medical history can visit and
see how we buggered it up. Remember, nothing in
there is worth money as money has been eliminated
in the new system so you should not get looting
and scrap men violating empty buildings. The new
"Cruise Ship" will be many smaller "boats"
specializing in medical subjects. They will have
a door at both ends and a virtual conveyor belt
where as soon as your doctor suspects something

you are sent there immediately and walk through the door that says "IN". Only the latest equipment will be installed. You will be diagnosed, operated on or treated there and then. When nothing else can be checked you walk or are helped out of the door that says "OUT". A persons abode will fit a hospital bed and all equipment and nurses and doctors will see to it you recover in your own home. This will slow down Super bugs and people dying from depression and demoralization, hospital food, being drugged up to the eyeballs by a student doctor, having to see other people treated or even die etc. The new centre should have a "matron" type with nobody above her. No fat cats, massively paid managers, trusts and other people who do not know anything about medical stuff. Drug companies state that the research for a new drug is what determines the price. The shares thing rears its ugly head here as we all know it is the shareholders wanting their dividends that determines the price. Most drugs have paid back their research money in the first few years but you do not see the price come down after that. In the new system if a drug is not being developed quickly enough, you just place the need for more researchers and buildings on the system and the researchers turn up and the buildings get built. All humans involved become a percentage closer to going to their Centre of Excellence choice for however many days they want.

Medical staff start their courses on their mobile devices at home once they have decided they want to be a doctor / nurse etc. They go to the actual Centres of Excellence treating the public for their work experience and specialize in one thing. It may be making the incision for the placement of a new lens in someones eye. That is what they become good at NOT the whole operation. Someone else takes the old lens out and someone else puts in the new lens etc. There will be use of highly magnified, highly accurate remote units for all surgery and effectively the expert could operate it from their abode. The short job system eliminates fatigue totally as the Doctor / surgeon only does one part of the operation they are really expert at. Some planets have a booth where if the inhabitant is feeling strange, they walk in and lay down. The experts on the "Internet" do the diagnosis and operation / drug giving. There may be 20000 people on the system diagnosing. The chances of 20000 trained diagnostic doctors getting a diagnosis wrong is next to nothing.

CHAPTER TWENTY-FOUR

24. Entertainment.

Just say you do not want to work and therefore sit at home. You will not be penalized for this like you are here. You can still ride anywhere on your buggy, eat from food sources and your abode is free. So is sound based entertainment, vision based entertainment and gaming based entertainment are free also. How does this work ?

Music industry. Now you get management companies signing someone who is good and promoting them, recording them and selling their records. The recent spate of TV programmes making stars out of wannabes follows a damaging path. The person singing in their shower is told by their parents, children , husband or the like that they sound good. They send in the form and arrive at the audition in their thousands. Their spirits and hopes are then shattered one by one until there is one left that gets signed and stays signed all the while the management company is raking in cash. They get next to nothing which in some cases is still much more than you or I would earn. The path is narrow and lots of pitfalls means most do not make it to the other end. Drugs, alcohol, being ripped off, debt, having to resell the house they bought for their old mum. The only person on the make is the fat asshole who owns the management company rubbing his hands in glee and buying houses / cars / boats at the expense of the singer. He says what is sung, he says what you look like, he says where you go etc. and when you fail you are dumped on a whim and the next frontsperson takes over. The "Singer" could also be fake and is actually put there as a front for the bigger operation. The fame is good to start with but always gets to all in the end. The legacy and past fame usually ruins the frontsperson for the rest of their life. If you buy a recording you are helping this.

The closest planet to us where they listen to noises for pleasure did it like this :

The person becomes interested in music and has free access to the whole planets created music past and present on their mobile device. They then visit The Centre of Excellence for that type of music where they have immediate access to the top recording gear, vocal coaches, instrument tutors and anything they like. They are taught songwriting skills but are encouraged to become their own creator and not become like others. For example, they will be taught how to use the instrument / recording system but not what to put on it. Every single sound ever created will be stored on the systems which can be used by you free as there are no royalties. It does not matter what noise you make even scraping your nails down a blackboard can be recorded and uploaded to the planetary database. There isn't someone telling you that you cannot upload it. What makes the difference is the people who listen to it. After upload to the music database it becomes available on everyones mobile device. A listener can listen to the song once where the uploader does not get anything. When a single being listens to the song twice the writer or up loader becomes a percentage closer to going to their Centre of Excellence be it a music centre or a beach centre or anything. This is their "Royalty" if you like. The better your song the higher it will get and the more people will listen to it. It is entered in a global "charts", "Hit Parade" instantly you upload it anyway. The public decide where it appears on the "chart" by listening to it. Everyone can contribute. As we know most songs these days are followed by the video. Most "songs" on other planets have a visual also. So this merges music with video so all is the same. The only difference is that you can do other things when the music video is on and do not have to look at the screen.

Films, TV programs and the like can all be created in the same way by going to the Centre of Excellence and setting up a like minded group of people and creating an idea which then becomes your series, film, one off program, documentary etc. There is no limit. If a person watches a trailer and likes it they can the watch it and the creators are rewarded with their choice of away time or even more visits to create more programs. If a person or group of people are producing a series and it is popular you will automatically have enough percentage points to stay there and produce it full time. Because the old world has been preserved on most intelligent planets there is no end of real scenery for your location filming.

A lesson we have learned here is not to let on who we actually are. Although your face will be shown in your music video you would have made up a "stage name" for yourself. You can remain relatively anonymous but your character can be famous. Just to say, newspapers will be scrapped mainly because they are no longer any good as chip paper but a waste of resources and will be all electronic. Journalists / reporters will not be able to post "untruths" about anyone. The "news" will be sourced and written by the individual and will not be allowed to be edited. Sorry to all you twisted humans who like to see people in a better financial position than you ridiculed and stamped upon but you cause it by buying the news. Its OK until it happens to you.

CHAPTER TWENTY-FIVE

25. Dating.

This is key to a beings happiness and cuts out a lot of other nasty things we would not think of. Here, we go about life hoping to meet the "one" and after years of looking we settle with someone who is a compromise due to time. Some go to bars and although people are content with their partner are they sure they have their soul mate ? The Human is becoming so sophisticated that a "rough fit" will not do.

Other planets similar to ours have a system based on elements of what we do here but leave nothing to chance and no stone unturned. The

resulting couple usually stay together forever.
Heres how. When a being reaches a certain age
their mobile device flags up all perfect matches
to what the being has registered on their mobile
device. It also knows your genetic makeup so can
match you genetically for possible problems or to
carry on a race. It shows those compatible in
your area and in the whole world so you can
assess if it is worth moving. Moving here and now
on this planet is a big problem due to money,
job, friends and the like. This has all been
eliminated in other words and you can move on a
whim taking your whole abode "lining" with you.
See chapter on abodes. You correspond with these
for a set period where it is then OK to meet. The
meeting period includes living together if you
both agree. At a set time you have to become
dedicated. This is not usually a problem because
the system gave you the match based on every
person on the globe. This match was based on
everything. All history on the mobile device so
if you both went to a Music based Centre of

Excellence this would be a factor, you would have put in what body type down to the finest detail, what looks you want, what hobbies, what music, what types of entertainment, what you do for relaxation, food preferences, and all the usual stuff like perfect height, weight, colour, hair, eyes etc. Here, if we had the system, the choice would be from Billions of people and the chance of getting the right one is maximized. The other thing dating sites here have tried is what type of relationship we want. So included in the preferences should be if you want a lifetime partner, one night stand, one week, one month and one planet has a "Honeymoon period" where a couple go their separate ways when this period ends and then go for another person who wants the honeymoon feeling and no more. At the moment here there are many different dating sites, charging a fortune, matching you to someone who likes "Walks on the beach" and that is it. It is all hit and miss.

I say above about body type down to the finest detail and I mean it. Some other worlds use body parts as a lure to the opposite sex to do what is necessary to promote the species. Here on Earth it is a fit body, good looks and sometimes penis size for women and for men, breast size, body shape, looks etc. These are guessable here but on the dating system could make all the difference to a mate being perfect and therefore less reason to become detached. Things like breast size, shape and nipple type being one. Penis shape, colour and type could make a slight difference to a woman. Long legs, short legs, teeth etc. I have heard there are some men who like the crooked teeth look some girls have in the far east. Some like the slight cross eyedness of some Chinese women. Everything and every slight detail has to be included to nudge forwards, even in the minutest detail, to that goal of the population being happy. When this happens, rape, paedophilia and a whole host of other stuff disappears. I am not suggesting that some girls may like to re-enact rape but in a survey I saw on the Internet in the 90s it came close to the top of a poll on girls fantasies. I suggest it goes in the category section of what type of relationship you want! This cuts out completely or virtually eliminates the rape by someone totally unknown as you have arranged it previously. Fantasy should be included as this seems to prolong relationships also. The fantasy that sticks out in my mind was a friend of mine who built a bar at his house and the bar was strangely mounted on a wooden floor boarded stage which had sound holes cut out of the step up. This boomed when you stood on it. One night when he was drunk he confessed that he was extremely turned on by the sound of a womans high heels on the stage moving about while he was making love to her. The rustling sound of her dress moving was another.

A Human here has the strange ability to move "down the ladder" whereas on not being able to get the top being of their dreams, after time resort to the next best thing and so on until they reach the bottom. This is inbuilt to carry on the human race and leave nothing to chance. The bottom is rape and paedophilia. Because you could not convince a member of the opposite sex to be with you the human will resort to controlling something they can't control normally using strength. There is no need to get to that point in the planetary system as a partner is always found. If no exact matches were on the system just expand to global search or take off the least important trait.

CHAPTER TWENTY-SIX

26. The End of the Universe.

We can explain most things and have theories about others. The question about where the universe ends is about the same as where the rainbow ends. The rainbow isn't actually there as we now know as it is just light passing through water droplets being split into its different colours as with a prism. Well, the universe isn't there either. You can spend millions of light years traveling and land on a planet and pick up rocks, meet other beings, and travel around touching things. You can go down the road to the shop, touch your pocket and change, touch the newspaper and drink the coffee and feel it go down hot but none of it is there as we perceive it. Our eyes are picking up light reflected off objects but they are not actually red or green etc. but have a surface that just reflects that wavelength or colour light. A person standing next to you will also agree something is green because they have been brought up and taught that an object reflecting that wavelength of light is the colour green. You could isolate him / her as a baby and teach them that green things are called red and they would think that.

The nitty gritty of it is what the building blocks of matter are actually made of. We know atoms now and know what they do and what each one looks like as a solid lump or a liquid or gas and we know the three building blocks of all atoms are Protons, Neutrons in the core and electrons orbiting. Adding these together in certain configurations makes different elements. This is basic Physics. But, an atom is 99% empty space if not less. The elements of the atom it is theorized are also made from smaller building blocks with probably hardly any actual solid material except the smaller particles that they are made from and so on. Eventually you cross the boundary from solid to effect or wave which does not exist as such but we know it is there because it is having an effect on its neighbours. Some say this only works for a while and when the big bang spreads its matter so far the distance between particles is so much that even the smallest one does not have any effect on its neighbour because it is too far away. So all is just a huge effect.

There are lots of different particles also that affect us like radiation and the most common is photons. These are light but are so small they act like a wave. A photon bouncing off a surface we call green just absorbed all the other photons hitting it but reflected the photon with the wave depicting green to us.

This seemed to be the probes weak point as it was still not sure what would happen if you were to travel in a straight line out and away from the big bang ? It has a theory that you would probably meet up with the debris from another big bang. But when do you call completely empty space nothing and how do you know direction if there are no points of light to navigate by and does nothing actually exist? The light also becomes bent near gravitational influences so over great distances the light you are trying to navigate by may not be where you think you see it.

So no "matter" actually exists. It is all electromagnetic effect. At the point where all "matter" breaks up and the particles become unable to influence their neighbour, is this "nothing". A single atom in space still has a great bond with its electrons and we have seen the energy released when you try to split one with the atomic explosions here on Earth. Will

the electrons eventually run out of energy and
stop orbiting the protons and neutrons ?

CHAPTER TWENTY-SEVEN

27. Future Problems.

Humans like to be occupied. We have a problem coming which has already started but if not checked no amount of laws are going to prevent bloodshed. We already have the religion problem where one religion wants all the others dead. But there is another. We are kept going by the vast amount of innovations coming out weekly. T.V. music and music players, telephones and mobile devices, computers and Internet, then the spate of reality T.V. programmes which have taken T.V. into a new realm of humans thinking this is all normal and I could go on. What has happened in other worlds is that all media and communication has been "hoovered up" into one device. The smart phone is here in a very simple form at the moment. Music genres are becoming harder to create and eventually you just will not be able to create anything new. People will be bored with T.V. and anyone with a Sky box will know with 600 channels you end up not bothering because most of it is repeats. We cannot now be amazed at the cinema as we have seen it all. What I am getting at is as soon as sound quality gets to a point where our ears just would not hear anything better and T.V.s, computer monitors and other visual devices reach a point where the resolution is so high that we will no longer be able to tell if one screen is better than another. Nothing new will come out. This is why the Centres of Excellence should be created for every aspect of life past and present. This gives the human something to look forward to. Going away to a nice hotel, doing things they like. We see areas of big cities where people have no money so therefore have nothing to do so they sit around on street corners bored to the point where they make their own entertainment. Gangs are formed. Left unchecked, the situation gets out of hand. People are bored with being polite even. There are even cases of "Dares" where a person has been dared by his mate to kill the next person they see just for fun and the milder version of hitting someone at random. As was said somewhere in the realms of this book, it used to be that everyone in a village said hello and any argument was normally tongue in cheek and laughed about. Now you can't even look at someone else without them becoming violent. If you say hello this is now classed as madness. This boredom will get a lot worse when we run out of things to entertain us.

As we have seen, war brings people together. Deep friendships are made on the battlefield and deep memories. This is obviously not the best solution. Events keep happening where I sit on the edge of my chair watching the news and am thinking this may be it. The Icelandic Volcano problem : If that went off with 10 times the power it would throw up enough dust to change things. The rise of Islam where the 1% of radicals holding the guns could easily control the 99% not holding them and wipe all "Non-believers" out. The 99% are suspiciously quiet like they want it to happen or are frightened to speak out. Well, now is your time to prove your religion is not enforced by threats and fear. Ebola : Unless we take the advice of the probe and its idea of a lock down of every planet member about once every year, we are going to get these viruses pop up more often and soon they will overcome all our attempts to drug them and by the evolutionary "trial and error" system will eventually get past and destroy the lot of us. Smaller life forms evolve much faster than us. The Arms Limitation Treaty is inadvertently destroying our method of "tipping off" big asteroids coming towards the Earth. We will need big Nukes. We are advertising ourselves in space with light and radio signals. It is very rare for a small planet to be harvested for minerals by a mineral collecting Mother Ship but not unknown. These do not know if there is life on a planet and just lower huge machines the likes we will not see for 1000s of years and scrape off the top 50 miles of the target planet. This is then processed as they proceed to another source and the huge "pellets" they produce are fired in the direction of their home planet which could have ceased to exist a million or two years before. These were not on the Universal Control Protocol now used by the top 250 odd and have been banned but not all have been found. When they have been spotted traveling in space, the ship that spotted it has been given orders to try to install a new control system but these have also evolved beings which have never been friendly. Wars have lasted 10000 years before. So if this happens any ship coming across one is allowed to waste resources and destroy it. All has been tried. Gassing : This is good because it allows the ship to be boarded a few hundred years later and the control system installed. Nudging : The ship would have put itself on a course for the next target while it was leaving the gravitational field of the last planet in the last solar system it visited. It will probably not have any fuel to waste on resetting a course or it has shut down for the journey so will not know it is off course. So you nudge it so that it changes its trajectory. A millionth of a millimetre, after a million years traveling could be millions of miles off course. The ship would have to wait a very long time to "run into" another solar system. Most systems are awakened by sensing the presence of gravity. The other problem you have is their possible defence mechanism. Get too close you could be destroyed yourself.

Back to The Earth. Our own moon could "steamroller" us as it alights on the Earths surface. It is said that it is moving away from us a few centimeters each year but this may change with a big asteroid hit. We may think a close shave by an asteroid is OK but one could hit the moon and knock it off course. Satellites : There are now so many satellites that one being knocked could spray the rest with debris doing 14000 mph. Remember the fleck of paint that detached itself from the space Shuttle? It cracked the windscreen on the next orbit. The Shuttle ran into it doing 14500 kph. Thats 4027 metres a second or roughly 4 kilometres a second.

I mentioned before that chimps were beginning to use weapons against other groups of Chimps now. All animals will eventually catch up with us. When they do there will be hell to pay. Cows will know we used to kill them in great numbers for our own food. They will be particularly upset with the Spanish if they are still here as they seem to taunt bulls for entertainment with a cape and then it does not stop there. Instead of letting the bull go back to the fields to fight another day the idiots kill the bull slowly. The bull is built similarly to us with lungs, a heart etc and just because it has a simple brain we think we can do what we like with it. The sign of an advanced and civilized peoples is shown by how they treat the species coming up behind them. Only ignorant peoples think the animals are there to do what they like with because they paid for them. Some idiots think animals were put here by their god for them to use. The probe warned me that all 250 planets in communication with each other will not look favourably at a species who are sharing a planet with less clever species and trying to control them, let alone kill them in great numbers, or even treat them as inferior. The probe said they never do anything about it because the original superior species always gets its payback from the ones evolving into intelligent species. What goes around comes around.

CHAPTER TWENTY-EIGHT

28. Previous Visits.

Don't think we have not been visited. There are those on the planetary "net" that agree not to contact a planet until it reaches a certain level of civilization. However, there are still the unknowns and some of these think it is good to intervene. Intervention has brought us forwards a few thousand years on several occasions. The probe I was in was part of a in between set of planets that decided to put an information system on each probe and while on a planetary surface doing its job it would open the doors and if there were beings that could come in and were of an advancement that they could decipher how to operate the system then this was a good enough level of civilization to be able to work out how to use the system. Our Voyager probe leaving the solar system after many years had a plaque on it depicting things on Earth and as I said before, was a primitive version of the probes information system. There is evidence of numerous encounters like mine where people have learned things but have not been able to put them to use because the means to build such items just didn't exist. Then there has been big interventions where the Romans used knowledge gained by persons unknown and a sudden surge in tech was witnessed like underfloor hot air heating, plumbing and water control devices and this all led to them building their Empire. As we know, Empires come and go and it is not worth starting them in the first place. The Greeks suddenly became good with numbers, the Egyptians were another matter.

Egyptians worshipped things in the sky like

the sun etc. I didn't ask questions about the Egyptians but whilst in conversation about other things, they kept appearing. The eye problem they all seem to have was derived from genetic engineering experiments by beings who were here in that area before the Egyptian period really set off. They were helped with machines to build the pyramids and the drawings depicting humans building the pyramids were after when they tried to build their own when the visitors had gone probably because they wanted their Kings and Queens to have a grave near their visitor "gods". If a ship is here for long it needs something to rest on so would have built structures for this purpose. Most ships that are sent to planets which have gasses around them and gravity because where you have mass you have gravity, will be built to be aerodynamic in all directions which is where our general saucer shape comes from. The big ships that came to Earth about this time had a docking system used on their Mother Ship that was pyramid shaped. The reason for the pyramid was because it was under you when you were alighting and if you had the reverse shape built in under the craft, it would align everything when you finally fitted totally over the pyramid. you could be quite a way off centre but could do nothing else but slide down to a perfect fit on the pyramid shape. They did not use a cone because there were various exit and entry sockets for services that had to be aligned also and whilst you were spinning up the discs your ship would not turn due to torque. You would think they would have all sorts of automatic guidance and tracking for this job but apparently, the less systems you have the less chance of failure especially over millions of years. The pyramids here should have some sort of tube or tunnel for the services entry and exit jobs also. The Egyptians would have thought these visitors were gods and worshipped them until something new to worship came along. Most simple beings try to worship something. It is like a cop out where you have found what you believe in and are not now open to new suggestions as your brain isn't big enough to cope with anything complicated. It was much easier to be governed by something than try to be your own person. There are people like this on Earth even today. Many beings have lost their lives as sacrifices because of other beings saying it was for the good and for our beliefs. The stupid Romans fed Christians to the lions in front of thousands of people for entertainment. Religion raising its ugly head again.

Back to visitors and in particular, landing sites. Theres a similar use for Stonehenge. A huge bowed bottomed saucer has to fit on a ring so as not to put pressure on the very bottom. At one stage I had the impression that the people who built all that stuff in Peru were all rescued off this planet as there was a problem with the water supply like the Earth was becoming hotter or to do with ash in the air.

CHAPTER TWENTY-NINE

29. Glossary of terms.

Glossary of Terms.

Just a few words used that might need
explanation and some daft truth stuff :

NET or PLANETARY INFORMATION SYSTEM = The
planets numbering around 250 that have
established a universal language and share info
over it including control protocols for most
ships in space.

PROBE = The device I was dealing with.

MOBILE DEVICE = Hand held device all planetary beings (and us) on the top 250 carry holding information about themselves and whatever they like. Has a percentage of memory dedicated to a planetary cloud containing backups of all devices, the government system and anything else that needs saving. Holds all access to entertainment systems also and can transmit visual data to the screens in ones abode.

PERCENTAGE REWARDS = This is what you get when you do services to your planet which then allows you to go to your choice of Centre of Excellence. The speed at which you arrive at this is controlled by resources like how many people want to go to the same Centre , how difficult your deed was and how many jobs there are left to do that particular time period. A percentage point in this context cannot be likened to money here because its value changes continuously.

CENTRE OF EXCELLENCE = A place where you earn the right to go by helping your planet which lays on free accommodation, food and entertainment or hobby relating to the activity of your choice. There are so many subjects that it would be impossible, even going to one a day, to cover all of them in one lifetime

TODAYS CHARITY = Charity means the Government can't afford it. In a future world what needs to be done is put on the jobs system and is done immediately and free earning the person doing the work a place in a Centre of Excellence of their choice.

TODAYS GOVERNMENT = Something you worm your way into to make a quick buck. A "Ship" that has become uncontrollable in a real world gets destroyed.

TODAYS HOSPITAL = Where they can be afforded they have two layers. From the head of a ward to the patients is the "business" layer and all above that is the "burden" layer. Uncontrollable "ship" comes to mind again. Destroyed by greedy "professionals", drug companies and equipment providers.

COUNTRY SYSTEM = A method of ring fencing your resources so that you can get money from other countries for them and then not realize the money used to defend them is double what the other country gave you. Does not exist on other planets.

MONEY = A method of restricting resources and extracting money using smoke and mirrors as taxes etc. so as to keep most of the money with the Toffs. They have kept actual money in your pocket because if it was stopped and everything went electronic, Officials backhanders would stop too.

TOFF = The top 1% of humans are Toffs. This

is based on something like an "Old boy network" made up of Government, Corporate, Bank and rich individuals who are allowed to enter the end of the money spectrum where most of it is kept. The top 1% hold 93% of the worlds money. All other people are "Commoners" and work only to provide the "Old Boy Network" with a river of money and are only given a pittance to just be able to survive and this is calculated in great detail to get close to the point where there is a rebellion but not quite reaching it. Their money is protected by the "Zombies".

ZOMBIE = In the real world these are those people taken from commoners who are told they are providing great service to their people but are actually there to protect the top 1% from loosing money. They take their instruction directly from the Government and abide by the laws written by them despite having the feeling what they are doing is wrong. In some cases they have been known to kill strangers in far away countries just to preserve oil money for Corporate Business who hold the strings of the Government in that country. In a situation where the Commoners are at the point where they are about to attack the government, the Zombies will be ordered to attack the Commoners. This has caused "Prepping" in the U.S. and some other places.

CORPORATE BUSINESS = Commoners are paid very little money to do the work, the profits go into huge salaries for the top brass and their taxes go to the Government but secretly come back as money paid in contracts where some of this then goes to the top brass as bonuses, pays the shareholders who are the only people who have spare money to afford them and can afford a broker to make sure these do not lose money which are the Toffs again, and commoners who try to buy shares and cannot afford a broker end up generally losing money which goes to the shares of those who can afford a broker i.e. The Toffs. Some Corporations are now so big they can influence the Government into not acting on things that kill humans.

SHARES = A money soaking method where commoners are allured into buying shares in a company and generally lose it where it then comes out as money on shares that have been brokered, sold into the pockets of those who can afford a broker, creating a slow and undetectable ebb of money into the Toffs bank accounts.

BRITISH GOVERNMENT = A covert organization taking money from its people and giving it to people from other countries whilst raking off some for themselves calling it "expenses".

TAX = A system of extracting money from Commoners to keep the Toffs coffers topped up so they never run out of things they fancy. A very small amount is used for things benefiting the Commoners being calculated at just enough to keep them from rioting.

INTEREST = Something the Government can't afford to pay on its loans now. Or anyone else.

AMERICAN GOVERNMENT = A group of headless chickens who every time they try to do something good end up digging themselves a deeper hole.

RUSSIAN GOVERNMENT = An exclusive club for organized crime which is shown by the company they keep in Dictatorships from dodgy countries.

AMERICAN PRIDE = TRUTH (Weapons of Mass Destruction.), LIBERTY (Guantanamo Bay.) and JUSTICE (O.J. Simpson.)

RACIST = A person who doesn't know they originated from Africa. We all did.

CHINA = A massive dragon slowly waking that is incredibly hungry.

ISIS = (Stands for, "I Said I'm Sorry".) An organization who twisted their rule book to say it was OK to kill but would actually be murdered by their own God if there was one. The organization is made up of people who have not been told that if they were to say and do nothing that their religion is having twice as many babies as all other religions so will take over anyway. The organization has done more to hurt Islam than at any other point in time. The name comes from saying sorry to all Muslims and Allah and to Islam in general, all those killed people they are going to meet on death instead of their 27 virgins. They will have to say sorry to Mohammad himself on the day they die who will be waiting to stamp on their heads for not listening to his teachings.

CIGARETTE = A drug left legal by the Government because it provides huge tax income to give to Foreigners.

PETROL = A method of extracting huge tax money from Commoners to give to Foreigners.

ALCOHOL = A mind altering substance not banned by the Government because the loss of revenue would cause Government bankruptcy and give M.P.s one less thing to do in Parliament bars.

SMALL BOY = One item offered to the top 1% as entertainment via secretive "rings".

GUN = An item that is a magnet for legislation despite not being responsible for killing as many people as most other things and are stigmatized by those making the law but who do not seem to realize they are protected by them.

POLICEMAN = A person tied down with red tape and paperwork whom the Government takes great glee in restricting with more laws. Useless against a criminal with a gun.

GUN LAW = Something slapped on law abiding citizens that does not affect criminals.

GUN BAN = Something slapped on a population to make sure the Government is not attacked so they can increase taxes and actually do whatever they like.

CRIMINAL = Person who can get what they want free and laugh at gun laws each time another comes out. They rest between jobs in a prison.

PRISON = A basic free hotel for criminals to rest in and learn new criminal trades whilst the Commoner (usually their victims) pays for their food, accommodation, free TV without a licence, clothing, university courses, Gym fees and security. In some Countries this does not apply. Prison means punishment by taking ones freedom. In the UK there are people committing crimes just to get to prison where they do not have to worry where the next meal is coming from.

BEDROOM TAX = A U.K. only tax on householders brought out because there is nothing left to tax.

CHINESE PERSON = A human originating from the area called China that thinks ground up parts of exotic creatures will cure them from their illnesses despite scientific proof to the contrary or existence of a better remedy. When outside their area they make good food for other Humans that does not resemble anything from their country. Well liked all over the globe.

JAPANESE PERSON = A Human originating from the area called Japan that thinks all other humans inhabiting the globe are stupid so could not possibly know they are killing Whales for food because they have their whaling ships sign written with the word "RESEARCH".

VOTING = Leaving the comfort of your own home to draw a cross on a piece of paper next to the name of a person you know is not going to change a thing.

More in version 1.2.

www.ingramcontent.com/pod-product-compliance
Lightning Source LLC
Chambersburg PA
CBHW060241290526
45789CB00001B/137